LEGAL ISSUES

FOR ENTREPRENEURS

LISA GORDON–DAVIS AND PETER CUMBERLEGE

JUTA

Legal Issues for Entrepreneurs
First published 2006 by Juta & Co.
Mercury Crescent
Wetton, 7780
Cape Town, South Africa

© 2007 Juta & Co. Ltd

ISBN-10: 0 7021 7276 6
ISBN-13: 978 0 7021 7276 2

Typeset in GillSans Light in 11pt on 15pt

Project Manager: Sharon Steyn
Editor: David Merrington
Typesetter: WaterBerry Designs cc, PO Box 1750, Hermanus 7200
Cover designer: WaterBerry Designs cc
Printed in South Africa by Shumani Printers

Preface and acknowledgements

This book has been written to assist and support entrepreneurs to steer through the myriad of laws, regulations and other legal requirements that are imposed on business by various levels of government.

Entrepreneurs need to focus on the business of business, and not on disentangling complex laws and regulations that they may or may not have to comply with. This book will assist you to identify legislation that is relevant and applicable to your emerging business.

The book is designed in as logical a sequence as is possible. Divided into three sections, it commences with those things you need to look into before you start your business, while you are setting it up and when you start operating.

Acknowledgements

The authors would like to thank the many government officials who assisted us by providing relevant information and input for this book.

The authors would also like to thank all Juta's editing and technical staff for providing invaluable assistance in making this book a reality.

Key to the icons

 Definition

 Activity

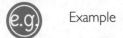 Example

 Explanation

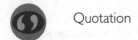 Quotation

 Tip

 Caution

 Thumbs up

Contents

Section 1:

Small business legal perspectives

1 Introduction to legal issues for entrepreneurs

1.1 Learning outcomes

After you have studied this chapter you should be able to

- determine whether your business meets the SMME classification,

- find out where to get support and guidance for your business idea,

- establish if there is an association that it may be worthwhile to join for business support, and

- gain an understanding of how this book will assist your business.

1.2 Introduction

Setting up your own business is not an easy task. However, it can be made a lot simpler if you are willing to learn and take advice from those who have, over many years, experienced the many challenges and pitfalls of entering the business world. For most people, starting an entirely new business is uncharted territory. It may offer great rewards, but at the same time it may confront you with equally high risks.

By ensuring that you stick to and follow some basic rules and requirements for setting up a small business, the risks can be reduced and the task made a lot easier. The Entrepreneurship series, covering such topics as basic finance, marketing, how to establish a business, and small business management, is specifically designed to reduce the risks and to help you put into place all of the basic requirements that will lay a solid platform for success.

Legal Issues for Entrepreneurs is no different. This book is designed to take you through all of the legal requirements of starting up a business. Being lawful from the outset will go a long way to ensuring the viability and future sustainability of your business and will eliminate any nasty and potentially costly surprises in the future.

An entrepreneur is a person who undertakes an enterprise, especially one with an element of risk.

The objective of this book is to assist you in reducing the impact of the 'element of risk'. Ensuring that your proposed business sets out on the right foot and complies with all legal requirements will undoubtedly get you off to a good start.

Legal Issues for Entrepreneurs will focus on small business, as most, if not all, of the successful, established, and profitable big businesses in South Africa started life as small enterprises. The use of the term 'small business' is very important, particularly in the context of South African legislation, as it defines the nature and size of the entity. Why is this important to know? Well, many of the laws in South Africa, promulgated either at national, provincial, or local level, make provision for the financing and support of small business while at the same time exempting them from certain restrictive or potentially costly legal provisions. It is therefore important for you to know from the outset whether or not your proposed business falls within the definition of small business.

1.3 What is a small business?

Small businesses are most commonly identified by the number of people employed in them. In general, a small or micro enterprise (SME) ranges in size from 5–50 employees. However, the official definition, provided by the *National Small Business Act, No 102 of 1996* is as follows:

A small business is defined as a separate and distinct business entity, including cooperative enterprises and non-governmental organisations, managed by one owner or more which, including its branches or subsidiaries, if any, is predominantly carried on in any sector or sub-sector of the economy mentioned in column I of the Schedule and which can be classified as a micro (very small), a small, or a medium enterprise by satisfying the criteria mentioned in columns 3, 4, and 5 of the Schedule opposite the smallest relevant size or class as mentioned in column 2 of the Schedule.

The schedule provides a sample of some of the business types contained in the *Amendment Act*, so it is important, depending on the type of business you are planning, for you to check the complete schedule.

To do that, you can go online to www.info.gov.za/documents/acts/2003.htm. Scroll down and click on 'Act No 26 National Small Business Amendment Act'. When you have opened it, scroll down to page 8. The schedule below is an example of the one contained in the *Small Business Amendment Act, 26 of 2003*.

Column 1 Sector or sub-sector	Column 2 Size	Column 3 Full-time paid employees	Column 4 Annual turnover	Column 5 Gross asset value (fixed property excluded)
Agriculture	Medium	100	R5m	R5m
	Small	50	R3m	R3m
	Very small	10	R0.5m	R0.5m
	Micro	5	R0.2m	R0.2m
Manufacturing	Medium	200	R51m	R19m
	Small	50	R13m	R5m
	Very small	10	R5m	R2m
	Micro	5	R0.2m	R0.1m
Retail	Medium	200	R39m	R6m
	Small	50	R19m	R3m
	Very small	20	R4m	R0.6m
	Micro	5	R0.2m	R0.1m
Catering & Accommodation	Medium	200	R13m	R3m
	Small	50	R6m	R1.0m
	Very small	20	R5.1m	R0.5m
	Micro	5	R0.2m	R0.1m
Finance & Business Services	Medium	200	R26m	R5m
	Small	50	R13m	R3m
	Very small	20	R3m	R0.5m
	Micro	5	R0.2m	R0.1m

Remember that it is important to categorise your business in line with the schedule in order to ensure that the various small business advantages and/or exemptions will apply to you.

We will use Jaque Khumalo's enterprise as an example to illustrate the basic legal requirements of a small business.

The Khumalo family are some of the most successful small farmers in the Tzaneen district. After matriculating, Jaque (one of the daughters) went to the city to study domestic science. She returned disillusioned when she was unable to find work. Jaque immediately started helping with the farm, which produces litchis, mangos, and other tropical fruit.

Since the fruit is seasonal and the sale of the fruit is the family's main source of income, it is hard going at certain times of the year. Jaque then hit on the idea of preserving fruit. In this way, the family would have something to sell all year round, and she could put her knowledge of domestic science to use. She started dreaming of an enterprise of her own, but realised that she needed more knowledge of the business world.

Jaque will have to determine the financial feasibility of her business, and, at the same time, investigate how to set it up so that it will be a lawful enterprise. She will have to investigate what form her enterprise must take, where it must be registered, and the lawful operating requirements, especially in terms of hygiene and food processing, licensing, tax requirements, employment requirements for the people she will employ to assist her in making the preserved fruit, and so on.

1.4 How the government views small business

The government aims to encourage entrepreneurship and the development of small businesses in order to grow the economy and create employment. It sets out to achieve this through such initiatives as black economic empowerment and small business exemptions. For example, SMMEs are exempted from paying the Skills Development Levy, and they are not required to establish safety committees under the *Occupational Health and Safety Act*.

Another example would be the Ministerial Determination for Small Business (*Government Gazette*, No. 20587, 5 November 1999) in terms of the *Basic Conditions of Employment Act*. This determination exempts small business, as defined, from a number of provisions contained in the *Basic Conditions of Employment Act* and covers such matters as overtime, the averaging of hours of work, and family responsibility leave.

Small business promotion and development is the responsibility of business, government, and labour. It is the key to substantial job creation and the redistribution of wealth. The government Strategy for Small Business Promotion was published in 1995 and has resulted in the creation of a National Institutional Framework for the creation of an enabling environment for small, micro, and medium enterprises (SMMEs) in South Africa. The Department of Trade and Industry's 'Centre for Small Business Promotion' is responsible for the implementation of the National Small Business Strategy.

1.5 Business support agencies

There are many organisations in South Africa that offer support to all types of business entities. Jaque would be able to approach any of these for help in starting and setting up her business. These organisations further recognise that, in order to combat the high unemployment level and its related problems, the small, medium, and micro-enterprise sector in South Africa needs to be developed.

> The Small Enterprise Development Agency (SEDA) will provide you with lots of information on business development.

Business centres are places where entrepreneurs and SMMEs can find support for their initiatives. These centres have been established to support business persons.

The Department of Trade & Industry (DTI) has a number of agencies, all of which will be able to assist small businesses in one way or another.

- Khula Enterprise Finance Limited
- The National Empowerment Fund (NEF)
- South African Women's Empowerment Network (SAWEN)
- Technology for Women in Business (TWIB)
- South African Micro-finance Apex Fund (SAMAF)
- The Companies and Intellectual Property Registration Office (CIPRO)
- The Enterprise Organisation's Small and Medium Enterprise Development Programme (SMEDP), and
- The Black Business Suppliers Development Programme (BBSDP)

> Find those centres closest to you and learn how they can assist you.

In order to identify and make the most of the potential of small business, the DTI recognises that support in the form of advice from specialist organisations is vital. The following topics cover the various support groups available to South African businesses. (You can find more information on small business support in chapter 3.)

1.6 Women entrepreneurs

Women are a key group in the South African business sector. South Africa recognises the invaluable potential and contribution that women can make to the economy. Inequities however do still exist, but the drive to acknowledge women formally in the work environment is crucial. Women can therefore access several established organisations (through the DTI website) in order to learn more about how to capitalise on their role in the South African economy. Jaque may find some specific support and guidance here.

Another key initiative that the DTI is involved in is SAWEN, a group of women entrepreneurs who are mobilised under the SAWEN umbrella in order to ensure that South African women entrepreneurs have a vehicle through which obstacles in business can be overcome.

The establishment of the South African Women Entrepreneurs Network (SAWEN) is a reaction to the fact that women entrepreneurs in South Africa continuously face a wide array of obstacles in starting, growing, and sustaining their own enterprises. This DTI initiative is a networking forum for individuals and organisations that are committed to the promotion and advancement of women entrepreneurs.

SAWEN will represent and articulate the aspirations of all women entrepreneurs (existing and potential) who operate within the South African SMME sector.

1.7 Young entrepreneurs

'The youth of our country are a valued possession of our nation. Without them, there can be no reconstruction and development programme. Without them, there can be no future.' *Nelson Mandela, May 1994*

This quote captures the need for South African business to recognise the critical role that young entrepreneurs can play in the economy of South Africa. The youth need to be mobilised and encouraged to contribute meaningfully to the South

African economy. The DTI website offers a range of useful links to organisations that have the expertise in this arena. Jaque may also approach any of the youth support organisations to support her emerging enterprise.

> If any of the associations mentioned meet any of your specific needs, contact them for further support and advice.

1.8 Financial support for SMMEs

Khula Enterprise Finance Limited is an agency of the DTI established in 1996 to facilitate access to finance for SMMEs. Khula provides assistance through various delivery channels. These include commercial banks, retail financial intermediaries (RFIs) and micro-credit outlets (MCOs). Through its Thuso Mentorship Programme, Khula also provides mentorship services to guide and counsel entrepreneurs in various aspects of managing their businesses.

Khula is a wholesale finance institution, which means that entrepreneurs do not get assistance directly from Khula but through the various institutions named above.

1.9 This book and your small business

The book is designed in as logical a sequence as is possible. It commences with those things you need to look into before you start your business, what you need to know while you are setting it up, and what you need when you start operating.

The content of this book is outlined below:

Section	Chapter	Topic	Content
1. Small business legal perspectives	1	Introduction	An overview of the content of this book and how it relates to your small business.
	2	Levels of law	How different levels of law affect small businesses.
	3	Red & green lights	Key research and decisions you need to make before starting up your business.
2. Business set-up	4	BEE	How black economic empowerment issues will affect your small business.
	5	Forms of business	An overview of the forms of business that you may choose for your small business. DTI recommends the use of close corporations for small businesses.

Section	Chapter	Topic	Content
	6	Property and premises	The legal considerations in getting your business premises up and running, including reference to relevant building codes.
	7	Registration to operate	The various types of registration that you need to run your business lawfully.
3. Business start-up	8	Operational contracts	A look at various types of contract that you are likely to encounter in a small business environment, including sale, lease, employment, franchising, and so on.
	9	Employment	The framework of employment legislation and how this applies to your business.
	10	Safety	An explanation of the framework of safety legislation in terms of general safety, and industry-specific regulations.
	11	Equity and development	How the Employment Equity and Skills Development Acts may affect you as a small business and whether you have to comply.

The three sections of the book relate to the phases of development that a business will go through as it moves from the conceptual stage to full operational status. These are:

- **Section 1: Small business perspectives** This section includes an explanation of how government views small businesses, as well as how the different levels of law affect small businesses. You will learn about critical decisions and their impact on the feasibility of your business idea, as well as any industry-specific requirements that may affect the establishment of your business.

- **Section 2: Setting up your business** This section is about setting up the business itself once you have determined whether the idea is legally possible. It addresses the legal side of start-up, including all licences and registrations.

- **Section 3: Starting up your business** This is the operational side of the business set-up, and ensures that your operation is lawful.

The rest of the chapters are as follows:

- **Chapter 2: Levels of law** All businesses in South Africa are required to implement and adhere to various forms of legislation. Business law is generated at three levels of government: national, provincial, and local government. This chapter will help you to understand the legislative process by identifying the various levels of government and how the Constitution provides for laws to be promulgated at each level.

- **Chapter 3: Research and investigation: Red and green lights** This chapter will ensure that, before you start up your new business, you will have asked and found out the answers to a number of critical questions. There are unfortunately certain legal barriers that may prevent you from starting up a particular business in a particular area or without a particular licence or permit. For example, if you do not have business rights on a property, you will not be able to operate a business from those premises. Each industry has different requirements for licensing, registration, and so on. This chapter will assist you in accessing the relevant information you need to start a business in a specific industry.

- **Chapter 4: Black economic empowerment (BEE)** A number of different industries have BEE charters and scorecards. In this chapter, BEE is explained and the effect of BEE legislation on your business is outlined.

- **Chapter 5: Forms of business** This chapter will provide you with important information on the various legal business structures you can adopt for your enterprise and provide you with information on the advantages and disadvantages of each. This will allow you to select the most appropriate legal structure for your small business.

- **Chapter 6: Property and premises** When operating a small business, the issue of premises must be addressed. In this chapter, the legal side of establishing or leasing premises is explored, including matters such as complying with the various building regulations and codes.

- **Chapter 7: Registration and licensing** Most businesses, more especially those that engage employees, will for various reasons be required to register with different national, provincial, and/or local authorities. This chapter provides guidance on a range of registrations and licensing requirements.

- **Chapter 8: Operational contracts** This chapter provides information on the legal aspects of contracts, leases, insurance, and other relevant issues.

- **Chapter 9: Conditions of employment** Employment law is a broad and complex topic. This chapter will provide you with the means to find and understand the different Acts and Regulations and how they relate to you and your business.

- **Chapter 10: Health and safety in the workplace** The Department of Labour has promulgated safety legislation for the protection of employees in the workplace. There are certain exemptions for small businesses in terms of how the workplace is regulated. This will be explained in Chapter 10.

- **Chapter 11: Employment equity and skills development** The development of people and skills training is vital for the growth of businesses and the economy. How this relates to business, to the role of small business, and to legal compliance with the *Skills Development Act* will be outlined in this chapter.

2 Levels of law

2.1 Learning outcomes

After you have studied this chapter, you should be able to

- describe the structure of government in South Africa,

- determine which levels of law may apply to your business operations, and where to find these sources of law, and

- explain the process of law making, and how this may affect your business.

2.2 Introduction

All citizens, as well as businesses in South Africa, are governed by a framework of legislation. It is important for you as a small business operator to have a clear understanding of what these laws are, and where they come from. This chapter will provide you with an overview of the levels of law that will apply to your business, and the process of how these laws were promulgated.

Law in South Africa is essentially divided into three categories or types:

- public or statutory law,
- civil law, and
- criminal law.

As a business operator, you may be affected by or have to deal with all three forms of law at some time or another. However, public or statutory law is the one that will impact on your business the most. As a result, this chapter will focus on public law as it applies to doing business in South Africa. Both civil and criminal law will be covered where and when necessary, throughout the book.

Statutory or public law is written law that has been drafted and published by the government and is underpinned by the South African Constitution. Laws made by the national or provincial parliaments are called *statutes* or *acts*. They are published in a government newspaper called the *Government Gazette*. An example of a national statutory law would be the *Tobacco Products Control Act, 83 of 1993*. This means it was the 83rd law passed in 1993. An example of a provincial law would be the *Gauteng Liquor Act, 2 of 2003*.

The Constitutional Court can declare any statute law invalid if it goes against the Constitution. Other courts can only declare less important laws invalid.

Parliament can grant the power to make less important laws to other groups of people or to a minister. Sometimes a statute gives power to a person (for example a minister) or a body (for example the Department of Trade and Industry (DTI)) to make regulations. An example would be how the DTI promulgated the *National Gambling Act*, which makes provision for each province to have a provincial gambling authority that lays down the laws within that province using the national legislation as the regulatory framework.

D   **Promulgation** is the process of making laws.

Provinces, towns, and cities are allowed to make their own laws that only apply to them. These are called ordinances for the provinces, or by-laws for the towns and cities. Examples of particular relevance to the hospitality industry are municipal health by-laws that expand on the national health regulations but have particular reference and application to a specific municipal area. Operators must always check with local authorities what their specific requirements are in addition to the national requirements. Section 1.6 of this chapter outlines in which fields provinces and municipalities have concurrent legislative and executive powers with the national sphere.

2.3 Levels of legislation

In order to ensure that you comply with all of the various statutory legal requirements for opening and operating a small business in South Africa, it helps to understand how they come about and which level of government is responsible for the administration, management, and policing thereof.

In South Africa, and in terms of our Constitution, we have three tiers of government.

Level	Promulgated by
National	Parliament
Provincial	Provincial legislature
Local or municipal	Municipalities

As a small business, you will be required to adhere to many of the national and provincial requirements, but in most cases the provisions or contents of these laws will be implemented, controlled, and policed by a local authority or municipality. Typical examples would be health and safety, both of which your local authority will administer in terms of your premises and operating procedures.

Jaque will have to find out what laws will affect her enterprise, and make sure that she meets all the requirements that these place on her business. These may be national laws such as the *Occupational Health and Safety Act*, or they may be local municipal by-laws relating to specific health issues in the district or area. It is important that she knows exactly which laws affect Jaque's Treats so that she does not break the law without realising it. If that happens, she may end up having to pay heavy penalties or fines, or even have to close her business.

Level	Legislation	Example
National	National acts and regulations	National liquor act and regulations
Provincial	Provincial ordinances and regulations	Provincial (retail) liquor acts
Municipal/local authorities	By-laws	Municipal by-laws: Liquor trading hours

1. Why should an entrepreneur know the levels of law and the process of law making?

2. How can you, as an entrepreneur, make sure that you comply with all levels of legislation that influence your enterprise?

We will now take a brief look at the structures of each of the three tiers of government and examine the legislative responsibilities of each level.

2.4 National government structures

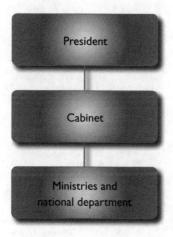

2.4.1 The president

The president is the head of state and leads the cabinet. He or she is elected by the National Assembly from among its members and leads the country in the interest of national unity and in accordance with the Constitution and the law.

2.4.2 The cabinet

The cabinet consists of the president, who is head of the cabinet, the deputy president, and a number of ministers, each with a different portfolio or responsibility. The president appoints the deputy president and ministers, assigns their powers and functions, and may dismiss them.

The president may select any number of ministers from among the members of the National Assembly, and may select no more than two ministers from outside the Assembly. The president appoints a member of the cabinet to be the leader of government business in the National Assembly.

2.4.3 Ministries and national departments

In order to ensure that the government is in a position to manage, administer and control all aspects of South African life, it consists of a number of ministries or departments. Each department has a minister and deputy minister in charge. Various sub sectors of each department are managed by directors-generals and or deputy directors-generals who in turn have a number of employees reporting to them.

The national government consists of the following departments:

Agriculture	Provincial and Local Government
Arts and Culture	Public Enterprises
Communications	Public Service and Administration
Correctional Services	Public Service Commission
Defence	Public Works
Education	Science and Technology
Environmental Affairs and Tourism	Secretariat for Safety and Security
Foreign Affairs	SA Management Development Institute
Government Communications (GCIS)	SA Police Service
Health	SA Revenue Service
Home Affairs	SA Secret Service
Housing	Social Development
Independent Complaints Directorate	Sport and Recreation
Justice and Constitutional Development	Statistics South Africa
Labour	The Presidency
Land Affairs	Trade and Industry
Minerals and Energy	Transport
National Intelligence Agency	Water Affairs and Forestry
National Treasury	

2.4.4 Parliament

The national Parliament is the legislative authority of South Africa and has the power to make laws for the country in accordance with the Constitution. It consists of the National Assembly and the National Council of Provinces (NCOP). Parliamentary sittings are open to the public.

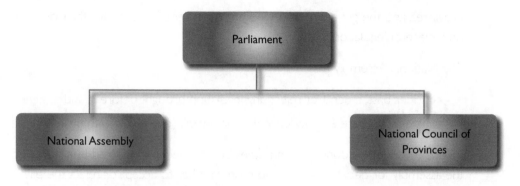

2.4.5 The National Assembly

The National Assembly is elected to represent the people and to ensure government by the people under the Constitution. It does this by choosing the President, by providing a national forum for public consideration of issues, by passing legislation, and by scrutinising and overseeing executive action.

The National Assembly consists of no fewer than 350 and no more than 400 members elected through a system of proportional representation. The National Assembly, which is elected for a term of five years, is presided over by a speaker, who is assisted by a deputy speaker.

The National Assembly, when exercising its legislative authority, is bound only by the Constitution and must act in accordance with and within the limits of the Constitution. It may make laws on any matter, but excluding matters referred to under Schedule 5 of the Constitution. Schedule 5 deals with functional areas of exclusive provincial legislative competence and covers matters other than national. Examples of these are provincial planning, provincial sport, veterinary services, libraries, and museums.

In addition, and in accordance with Schedule 4 of the Constitution, certain matters are decided upon at both national and provincial level. This is described as functional areas of concurrent national and provincial legislative competence.

An example would be the administration, management, and control of liquor in South Africa. The National Assembly was responsible for drawing up and legislating the *Liquor Act, 59 of 2003* which, broadly speaking, deals with the manufacturing, wholesale, and distribution of liquor in South Africa. Thereafter, each of the nine provinces is responsible for the licensing of the retail sales of liquor in South Africa; that is, the liquor stores, hotels, and restaurants that sell liquor direct to the public.

What usually occurs is that the various national government departments draft legislation for consideration by the National Assembly, the National Council of

Provinces, and the general public, who are often requested to give their opinion on a piece of legislation.

The National Assembly may

- consider, pass, amend, or reject any legislation brought before it, and
- initiate or prepare any law, except a money bill (one to do with finance).

Most of this work is done in committees before the bill is referred to a sitting of the assembly for debate and for a vote on whether to accept or reject the bill.

2.4.6 The National Council of Provinces

The National Council of Provinces represents the provinces to ensure that provincial interests are taken into account in the national sphere of government. It does this mainly by participating in the national legislative process and by providing a national forum for public consideration of issues affecting the provinces.

The NCOP consists of 54 permanent members and 36 special delegates, and aims to represent provincial interests in the national sphere of government. Delegations from each province consist of 10 representatives. The NCOP gets a mandate from the provinces before it can make certain decisions. It cannot, however, initiate a bill concerning money, which is the prerogative of the Minister of Finance.

2.5 Provincial government

In accordance with the Constitution, each of the nine provinces has its own legislature consisting of between 30 and 80 members. The number of members is determined in terms of a formula set out in national legislation. The premier is elected by the provincial legislature. The members are elected in terms of proportional representation. Decisions are taken by consensus, as happens in the national cabinet.

The legislative authority of a province is vested in its provincial legislature, which may pass legislation on any matter listed in Schedule 4 and Schedule 5 of the Constitution.

The provincial government may pass laws on

- any matter that is expressly assigned to the province by national legislation,
- any matter for which a provision of the Constitution envisages the enactment of provincial legislation, and
- may assign any of its legislative powers to a municipal council in that province.

A provincial legislature is bound only by the Constitution and, if it has passed a constitution for its province, also by that constitution. A provincial legislature may recommend to the National Assembly legislation concerning any matter outside the authority of that legislature, or in respect of which an Act of Parliament prevails over a provincial law.

Schedule 4 of the Constitution lists specific areas of concurrent national and provincial legislative competence and includes such areas as

- agriculture,
- casinos,
- consumer protection,
- health services,
- housing,
- language policy,
- nature conservation,
- pollution,
- road traffic regulation,
- tourism, and
- welfare services.

Schedule 5: Part A of the Constitution deals with exclusive provincial powers and includes such areas as

- ambulance services,
- liquor licenses,
- provincial planning,

- provincial sport,
- provincial roads and traffic, and
- veterinary services.

Schedule 5: Part B of the Constitution deals with specific areas of concurrent provincial and local government legislative competence and includes such areas as

- beaches,
- cleansing,
- control of undertakings that sell liquor to the public,
- fencing and fences,
- licensing and control of undertakings that sell food to the public,
- markets,
- municipal roads,
- noise pollution,
- public places,
- refuse removal,
- street trading, and
- traffic and parking.

2.6 Local or municipal government

Towns and cities are allowed to make their own laws that will then only apply to them. These are called by-laws. Many local laws will impact on the operations of a small business, in terms of things like licensing, building regulations, fire regulations, health regulations, trading requirements, and so on.

As a small business owner, it is important for you to understand the areas of law that the local government has the power to promulgate and enforce. You will have to ensure that you know what the local laws are, as the local government structure (municipality) will enforce these.

Examples of particular relevance to most businesses are municipal health by-laws that expand on the national health regulations but have particular reference and application to a specific municipal area.

The recognition of local government in the Constitution as a sphere of government has enhanced the status of local government as a whole and of municipalities in particular, and has given them a new dynamic role as instruments of delivery.

The Constitution provides for three categories of local government described as municipalities:

- Category A (metropolitan municipalities)
- Category B (district municipalities)
- Category C (local area municipalities)

It also determines that Category A municipalities can only be established in metropolitan areas such as Johannesburg, Durban, Cape Town, Tshwane (Pretoria), Ekurhuleni (East Rand), and Nelson Mandela (Port Elizabeth). South Africa has six metropolitan municipalities, 231 local municipalities, and 47 district municipalities.

The national and provincial governments must assign to a municipality, by agreement and subject to various conditions, the administration of a number of matters such as those contained in Schedule 4 Part B of the Constitution. This includes such areas as

- air pollution,
- building regulations,
- electricity and gas reticulation,
- fire-fighting services,
- local tourism,
- municipal planning,
- municipal health services,
- municipal public works,
- storm water management,
- trading regulations, and
- water and sanitation services.

The provincial government must assign to a municipality, by agreement and subject to various conditions, the administration of a number of matters such as those contained in Schedule 5 Part B of the Constitution. These include such areas as

- beaches,
- cleansing,
- control of undertakings that sell liquor to the public,
- fencing and fences,
- licensing and control of undertakings that sell food to the public,
- markets,
- municipal roads,
- noise pollution,
- public places,
- refuse removal,
- street trading, and
- traffic and parking.

As you will note from the above, the local authority, although working in tandem with both the national government and its particular provincial government, deals with many issues that impact on business in a town or city. Such matters as fire, safety, building, trading, and health services are all issues that concern and affect any business in any town or city.

For this reason, it is important for all prospective or established business owners to check with their local authorities about the specific requirements they are required to adhere to when opening or running a business.

2.7 The process of law making

The national government, through the various departments, will decide that a particular piece of legislation is required. The department will usually do some initial research and then draft a document for approval by the legislature. Depending on the type and likely impact of the legislation, the legislature may decide that public input is required and that the document must go through a process of consultation with both public and private sector stakeholders. They may decide to commence the process at what is called the 'green paper' level. The green paper will be a very broad draft which, after input by various stakeholders, will be amended, expanded upon, and republished as a 'white paper'.

Once again, both public and private sector stakeholders will be given an opportunity to comment on the amended draft. Amendments, alterations, and additions will be made and a bill published. Both the National Assembly and the National Council of Provinces will then table the bill in Parliament for debate and discussions. During this period, the public will be given a final opportunity to comment. Finally, the bill will be approved by Parliament and sent to the president's office for his approval and promulgation as an Act

Although a particular piece of legislation may go through the green paper, white paper, and bill stages before becoming law, in most cases the proposal will commence at the draft bill stage.

Most, if not all, of the Acts passed will have what are termed as Regulations attached to them. Whereas the Acts are invariably very broad based and spell out the purpose, application, interpretation, management, and administration of a particular subject, the Regulations essentially spell out what we as citizens are required to do, how the provisions of the Act should be followed, and how the Act should be implemented and policed by the various tiers of government.

What	Action	Who
Green paper	Drafted and published for comment	Relevant ministry
White paper	Drafted and published for comment	Relevant ministry
Draft bill	Gazetted and published for comment	
Bill	Tabled in Parliament, goes to committee for consideration, then returned to Parliament for discussion and approval	National Assembly National Council of Provinces committees
Act	Bill signed	State President

Below is a selection of Acts of legislation that that have been promulgated by the national legislature over recent years. Most of these Acts and many others will have either a direct or indirect impact on your business both now and into the future.

It is important to note that many of these Acts will have been amended over the years and are provided solely as an example of the varied and diverse types of legislation passed by the national Parliament.

- *Architectural Profession Act, 44 of 2000*
- *Basic Conditions of Employment Act, 75 of 1997*
- *Broad-Based Black Economic Empowerment Act, 53 of 2003*
- *Companies Amendment Act, 35 of 2001*
- *Compensation for Occupational Injuries and Diseases Act, 130 of 1993*
- *Competition Act, 89 of 1998*

- *Employment Equity Act, 55 of 1998*
- *Engineering Profession Act, 46 of 2000*
- *Environmental Management Act, 107 of 1998*
- *Fire Brigade Services Amendment Act, 14 of 2000*
- *Firearms Control Amendment Act, 43 of 2003*
- *Gambling Act, 33 of 1996*
- *Health Act, 61 of 2003*
- *Income Tax Act, 28 of 1997*
- *Labour Relations Act, 66 of 1995*
- *Landscape Architectural Profession Act, 45 of 2000*
- *Liquor Act, 59 of 2003*
- *Local Government: Municipal Property Rates Act, 6 of 2004*
- *Long-Term Insurance Act, 52 of 1998*
- *Occupational Health and Safety Act, 85 of 1993*
- *Prevention of Illegal Eviction from and Unlawful Occupation of Land Act, 19 of 1998*
- *Promotion of Access to Information Act, 2 of 2000*
- *Promotion of Equality and Prevention of Unfair Discrimination Act, 4 of 2000*
- *Public Holidays Act, 36 of 1994*
- *Road Accident Fund Act, 56 of 1996*
- *Short-term Insurance Act, 53 of 1998*
- *Skills Development Act, 97 of 1998*
- *Skills Development Levies Act, 9 of 1999*
- *Small Business Act, 102 of 1996*
- *Tobacco Products Control Act, 83 of 1993*
- *Town and Regional Planners Amendment Act, 3 of 1995*
- *Unemployment Insurance Act, 63 of 2001*
- *Unemployment Insurance Contributions Act, 4 of 2002*
- *Water Act, 36 of 1998*

Looking through the above enactments promulgated over recent years, it is clear that business cannot ignore national legislation. Throughout this book, we will be looking at various enactments, the manner in which they will affect what you are required to do, and how you should apply them to your business.

<table>
<tr><td>**D**</td><td>**Enactments** are laws.</td></tr>
</table>

Below are a few examples of provincial enactments as well as by-laws that have been approved by various local or municipal authorities.

This is a sample of a few provincial laws:

- Western Cape Tourism Act, 2004
- KwaZulu-Natal Tourism Amendment Act, 7 of 1998
- KwaZulu-Natal Tourism Act, 1996
- KwaZulu-Natal Gambling Amendment Act, 11 of 1998
- Eastern Cape Liquor Act, 10 of 2003

These are examples of a few local by-laws:

- City of Johannesburg Metropolitan Municipality – Metered Taxi, Minibus, and Bus By-laws
- City of Johannesburg Metropolitan Municipality – Public Health By-laws
- City of Cape Town – By-Law Relating to Dumping and Littering
- City of Cape Town – By-Law Relating to Filming
- City of Cape Town – By-Law Relating to Environmental Health

2.8 Self-evaluation

1. What kinds of law are found in South Africa?
2. What are the three levels of legislation in South Africa?
3. List three of the structures into which the national government is divided.
4. Explain in your own words what a green paper is.
5. Thabo is setting up a restaurant and bar. What enactments are likely to affect him from a national, provincial, and local level? Have a look at the list provided in this chapter and see the range of the laws that he will have to comply with.

Research and investigation: Red and green lights

3.1 Learning outcomes

After you have studied this chapter you should be able to

- determine whether your business idea is legally acceptable,

- research the industry requirements that your business will have to conform to,

- locate an industry association that may be able to advise you on your business start-up and legal requirements, and

- determine what municipal compliance your business may have to meet.

3.2 Introduction

This chapter is designed to assist you in establishing from the beginning, and solely from a legal perspective, whether or not you should proceed with your small business idea and what key factors you should take into account when deciding on the type and location of premises best suited to your needs. In addition, this chapter provides information on how best to access the required information, what the possible legal requirements may be, and who to contact while researching your proposed business.

Even before setting up your business plan, and certainly before you incur any major expense, it would be wise for you to establish the following:

- Am I legally permitted to run such a business in South Africa?
- Am I required to have any personal qualifications in order to do so?
- Are there any restrictions as to where I locate my business?

- Am I required to register with anyone?
- Am I required to have a certain type of premises?
- Do I need a licence or licences to operate?

These are the kinds of question that Jaque will have to both ask and answer to determine whether her business idea is lawfully possible. It is no use if she goes ahead with her idea only to discover, after investing in product development, bottling machines, label design, and so on, that she will not qualify for the right kinds of licence in the area in which she wants to run her small business.

It is therefore really important for Jaque, or any other entrepreneur, to ask the right questions, and to get answers to these questions before investing any money in the potential enterprise. At this stage, an investment of time is the most important and could save a significant amount of both time and money later.

Research is the key. If you establish everything you need to know before starting up the business, you will not only have peace of mind but you will in all probability have saved yourself a lot of unnecessary expenditure.

Spending one or two months investigating every aspect of your proposed business will probably be one of the most valuable and significant investments you are likely to make. A lawful and successful business is always founded on solid and in-depth research.

What can possibly go wrong, you might ask? 'I have talked to my friends and they think I have come up with a great idea. Now all I need to do is find premises and open up my business.'

Let's take a quick look at some examples of what can go wrong if you have not done your homework.

Example 1

Let's say, for example, you are thinking of opening a pharmacy. You may believe that all you are required to do is to lease or rent premises, buy stock from the suppliers, and open your doors to the public. Nothing could be further from the truth.

Unfortunately, right from the outset you are going to experience your first challenge. No sooner have you signed your lease, set up the premises, purchased shop fittings and furniture, etc., than you discover that the pharmaceutical manufacturers will not supply you with any products. Their first request is for a copy of your registration certificate from the Pharmacy Council. As a result, you contact the Council to enquire about the registration process and this is where it all goes wrong.

You do your homework and carry out research long before you look to leasing premises or purchasing any products. You pick up the phone and call the Pharmaceutical Society of South Africa in Johannesburg and in two minutes discover that you going to have to spend around six years obtaining the qualifications required to become a pharmacist in order to register with the Pharmacy Council. No harm done, and only the cost of a phone call. Decision? Either you then decide to invest in six years of study to achieve your goal or it's back to the drawing board and a change of direction.

Example 2

Perhaps you are looking to open a restaurant and have found what you believe to be the perfect location. You set everything up, spend a lot of money on equipment, furniture, and fittings, employ your staff, open to the public, and start operating. A key part of your plan is then to apply for a liquor licence in order to compete with the restaurants around you and increase your customer base. So, having committed yourself totally by opening the business, you make an application for a liquor licence and to your dismay it is declined. As a result, and right from the outset, you will be trading at a disadvantage to most of your competitors in the area.

Long before you set up your business and sign a lease for the premises, you decide to do your homework and carry out in-depth research. During this research, you visit the Provincial Liquor Authority and discover that the premises you earmarked will unfortunately not be suitable. The authorities point out that one of the provisions in the liquor legislation requires that the licensed premises should not be located within a kilometre of a school or church. Unfortunately, the perfect location you had earmarked is opposite a church and there is a school about five hundred metres down the road.

No harm done, and no cost incurred. As a result of having spoken to the provincial liquor authorities, you have established the exact requirements for obtaining a licence and can therefore ensure that the premises you are looking for meet all the requirements.

Example 3

 You decide to open a butchery. You lease the premises, purchase all of the operating equipment and shop fittings, spend a lot of money with builders making alterations to the premises, employ staff, purchase your stock, and open to the public. Someone then tells you that you must apply for a trading licence, which you do by approaching the licensing department at your local authority.

This is where it all goes wrong. First, an inspector from the health department visits and you discover that the premises fall well short of the health standards required to prepare and sell meat and food to the public. Then along comes the fire inspector and once again the premises do not meet the safety regulations and you discover that you are going to have to make a number of alterations at considerable cost.

Then, as if you don't have enough problems, along come the town planners: they deliver the killing blow by informing you that the area you have chosen, and therefore the premises, is not zoned for the sale of meat and food and that you will have to close down immediately.

During your initial research, you discover that you are required to obtain a trading licence to open the proposed butchery. You immediately visit your local authority and they explain exactly what is required. They tell you all about the health, safety, and zoning requirements. No harm done, and no cost incurred. Now you know exactly what you are looking for. You know in what areas the premises should be located, and you have a good idea as to both the health and safety requirements the premises should meet before you even consider signing the lease.

3.3 Accessing information

Although this book covers most of the generic legal requirements for running a small business in South Africa, many business types will be required to adhere to industry-specific legislation or even product-specific legislation, and this information is more difficult to access.

For example, if you intend opening a butchery, you are going to be required to adhere to very strict and specific health regulations. If you intend opening a shop and selling gas, you will be required to adhere to very specific fire and safety regulations. These regulations are industry or product specific and may not necessarily apply to another type of business.

We have clearly established that the need for in-depth research is important before implementing your proposal. So, how do you go about this research? How do you find out what you need to know?

Where to start?

There are at least three distinct steps you can take, together with a fourth option, which would be a 'nice to have' if you have any contacts in the industry you intend being part of.

- First identify, contact, and if possible visit the association, council, or organisation that represents the industry and sector that you are interested in.

- Second, visit your local authority or municipality and discuss your ideas with the various department heads. Start by asking to see a representative of the town or city planning department.

- Third, carry out some research online if you have a computer and are Internet connected. In addition, visit specific small business organisations that can assist you with relevant information.

- Fourth, and for as long as you have a few contacts, get in touch with someone you know who is already running a similar business.

3.3.1 Associations, councils, or organisations

There can be no doubt that your initial research will be extremely important in terms of the future success of your proposed business. The first step that we recommend is that you locate and contact the appropriate association, council, or organisation that operates in the sector of interest to you.

There are at least 30 industry sectors in South Africa, most of which will have formed a national or regional body that represents the specific interests of that particular sector. Examples of the various industry sectors are:

- Agriculture,
- Agroprocessing,
- Arts and Crafts,
- Automotive,
- Beverages,

- Building and Construction,
- Chemicals,
- Clothing,
- Energy,
- Engineering,

- Financial Services,
- Fishing,
- Food,
- Footwear,
- Forestry,
- Furniture,
- Information and Communication Technology,
- Jewellery,
- Leather,
- Machinery,
- Metals,
- Mining,
- Other Services,
- Paper and Paper Products,
- Pharmaceuticals,
- Plastic Products,
- Print and Publishing,
- Property,
- Recycling,
- Rubber Products,
- Textiles,
- Tourism, and
- Wood Products.

Most of these sectors, as mentioned above, will have a representative body. Typical examples of such industry-specific organisations would be:

- Associated South African Travel Agents ,
- Association of Auto Component & Allied Manufacture,
- Association of the Pulp and Paper Industry of SA,
- Building Industries Federation of SA,
- Economic Society of South Africa,
- Electrical Contractors Association (SA),
- Federated Hospitality Association of South Africa,
- Information Technology Association,
- Institute of Commercial & Financial Accountants,
- Insurance Institute of South Africa,
- Pharmaceutical Society of South Africa in Johannesburg,
- Public Accountants' and Auditors' Board
- Recording Industry of South Africa,
- S A Institute of Chartered Accountants,
- S A Property Owners Association,
- South African Landscapers Institute, and
- Tourism Business Council of South Africa

Please note that this list is by no means exhaustive.

Establish which organisation you should contact and you will find that, in most instances, they will be prepared to give you a brief outline of what is required, or alternatively they will put you in touch with someone who can help.

In some instances, you may be required to become a member of the organisation before they will provide you with the required information. Before doing this, it is suggested that you ascertain the fees and at the same time establish that they will definitely be able to provide you with all of the information you might need.

Do

Find out which associations or organisations are active in your industry sector. Completing the following table will help you with your research:

Organisation	What they do	Contact details	Contact person

3.3.2 Local authorities or municipalities

In terms of the South African Constitution, many aspects of business are regulated, administered, and controlled by local councils or municipalities. Typical examples would be building regulations, fire-fighting services, noise pollution, trade licences and permits, health services, water, and sanitation services.

Additional matters such as the display of advertising, the sale of food or liquor, fencing and fences, and street trading are also controlled by the local authorities.

For example, a typical health by-law would cover such matters as hazards and nuisances; hazardous uses of premises; sanitary services including sewage system and toilets; private sewage works; water supply, boreholes and wells; 'offensive trades' and storage of waste; hairdressing, beauty, and cosmetology services; second-hand goods; accommodation establishments; dry-cleaning and laundry businesses; swimming pools and spa-baths; nursing homes; child-care services; keeping of animals; pet shops and parlours; offences and penalties.

It will be imperative that you make contact with your local authority at some stage prior to commencing your business in order to verify all of the various requirements pertinent to your proposed business.

Every local authority will have various departments that deal with specific local issues. For example:

- The health department will give you all the information you might need in terms of the most appropriate premises and what facilities you may be required to put in place.

- The fire services will assist you in understanding the various safety requirements and equipment required to protect your premises, your staff and the public.

- The town planning department will guide you as to where you will be permitted to open your business and the style and type of premises that will be appropriate.

- The licensing department will assist you in determining what, if any, licences you may need.

- The water and electricity department will advise you on connection requirements, services, and costs.

In order to assist you a little further, we will take a closer look at some of the functions and responsibilities of a few of the departments in local government.

Local municipality's town planning department

The local municipality's town planning department will advise you on the zoning or land use of a particular property or premises. They will be able to tell you where you can and where you can't operate the type of business you are planning. If the proposed activity is permitted, this is referred to as a 'primary use right'. If the zoning does not make provision for the intended use, it would then be handled by the respective council as a 'departure' or 'special consent' use. This would mean that you will be required to make application for a change in the consent use. The town planners will be able to tell you whether or not such an application will be necessary and successful.

When the city council is required to consider a 'departure' or 'special consent', the process can take anything up to three months and in some cases requires that advertisements are placed in daily newspapers covering the business's intention to conduct its particular business activities. Objections from the public are then heard by the board before a 'departure' or 'special consent' is granted.

Any person who contravenes the *Land Use Planning Ordinance No. 15 of 1985* will, in all probability, be found guilty of an offence and will be liable to a fine and/ or imprisonment.

It is also the responsibility of the town planners to design and maintain the physical, social, and economic characteristics of a particular area. In so doing they will consider

- the physical, social, and economic characteristics of any neighbouring areas,
- the distribution, increase, movement, and urbanisation of the population in that area,
- the natural and other resources, and the economic development potential of that area,
- the existing infrastructure, such as water, electricity, communication networks, and transport systems in that area, and
- the general land use pattern and sensitivity of the natural environment in that area.

Health department

The local department of health is required to strictly enforce the various provisions of the national *Health Act* and is therefore responsible for ensuring that hygienic and clean conditions are maintained in the area in order to prevent a health nuisance, any offensive condition, or any water or primary health condition that may be harmful or dangerous to the public.

The department will be able to advise you on the type of premises that would be most suited to your business. They will be able to give you an idea as to the types of building materials or shop fittings that may be required and how best to accommodate the ablution needs of your staff and the public.

If you intend selling food to the public, they will tell you all about the requirements and application procedures concerning the 'Certificate of Acceptability for Food Premises'.

Fire department

The fire department is required to carry out a thorough inspection to ensure that the premises comply with all the safety regulations and are not a fire hazard. They will be quite happy to give you an idea about the type and suitability of premises and will explain all of the required safety features as well as the fire and safety equipment that will be required to protect you, your premises, your employees, and the public.

As can be seen from the above, it will undoubtedly pay you to contact your local authority. Find out who you should speak to and make arrangements to visit.

> It would be a good idea to make a list of questions that you would like to ask so that you don't miss anything.

3.4 Small business organisations

Having made contact with the various industry associations, and after having met with a representative of the local authority, it is suggested that you now make contact with one or more of the organisations that are set up specifically to provide relevant information and assistance to small business owners.

3.4.1 Small Enterprise Development Agency (SEDA)

A very good example would be the Small Enterprise Development Agency (SEDA) website, which you can visit at www.seda.org.za.

SEDA was established through the Department of Trade and Industry in December 2004 in terms of the national *Small Business Act*. The mandate of SEDA is to design and implement a standard national delivery network that must uniformly apply throughout the country. Its role includes the support and promotion of SMEs and cooperative enterprises, particularly those located in rural areas. It is highly recommended that you contact SEDA and obtain as much information as possible from them before you open your new business.

3.4.2 National African Federated Chamber of Commerce and Industry (Nafcoc)

Another organisation you could contact would be the National African Federated Chamber of Commerce and Industry (Nafcoc). They have recently opened four business service centres for SMEs. These centres have been established in Sandton, Soweto, Mpumalanga, and the Free State.

These centres will provide services to both member and non-member enterprises within each area. The support services will include, among others, research facilities, import-export information and linkages, and national and international tenders, as well as economic data analysis to help SMEs understand the regulatory environment in the country. A further part of their strategy is to foster new business ventures and help identify and expand new enterprises into different industries.

3.4.3 The Department of Trade and Industry

You should also make contact with the Department of Trade and Industry and they will assist you or alternatively recommend others who can assist you with regard to the legal requirements for many business types. Examples of these various business types would include

- agriculture,
- bakery,
- bed and breakfast,
- beekeeping,
- biotechnology,
- brick making,
- call centres,
- catering,
- chickens and poultry,
- cleaning services,
- coffee,
- debt collecting,
- diaper manufacturing,
- glass recycling,

- food processing,
- furniture making,
- hair care and cosmetics,
- hydroponics,
- Internet café (cyber café),
- low-cost housing,
- marula processing,
- mushroom growing,
- retailing,
- security,
- small-scale mining,
- soap making, and
- vehicle tyre recycling

3.4.4 Chambers of commerce

It would also be an idea to visit your local chamber of commerce or business centre as they will undoubtedly be able to assist you. They will not only have a good idea about the various legal requirements but will be in a position to put you in touch with other persons or organisations that can assist you still further.

 If you investigate at least three of the four options listed above and research the various legal requirements associated with your proposed business, you will be off to an excellent start. Remember to do this research before you start incurring any major costs.

3.5 Self-evaluation

1. Compile a file of information that you will use for the start-up of your business. Organise it in different sections that make sense to you. For example: SARS, municipality, business registration, and so on.

2. List at least three different municipal departments that Jaque may have to deal with in establishing her enterprise.

3. How will an association or organisation be able to help an entrepreneur determine whether his or her business idea is legally possible?

4. With what broad requirements are the following services or service providers required to comply?

Accommodation	Renting of hotel rooms, flats, guesthouses
Household services	Repair services for household appliances, cleaning of houses, gardening services
Recreation	Cinemas, holiday resorts, video-game arcades, sports clubs
Personal services	Barbers, beauticians, florists, dry cleaners
Medical services	Physiotherapists, dentists, optometrists
Educational services	Typing courses, computer courses, small business management courses
Professional services	Attorneys, accountants, consultants
Insurance and financial	Insurance brokers, real estate agents, banks
Transport services	Taxis, delivery services, transport contractors
Communication services	Paging services, cellular phone companies

Section 2:

Business set-up

4 Black economic empowerment

4.1 Learning outcomes

After you have studied this chapter, you should be able to

- make a business case for BEE,
- estimate your current BEE rating against the key indicators, and
- plan how to improve your rating where possible.

4.2 Introduction

Economic empowerment is an integral and important part of South Africa's transformation process, encouraging the redistribution of wealth and opportunities to previously disadvantaged communities and individuals, including black people, women, and people with disabilities. The empowerment process has been identified as crucial to the future viability of the country's economy.

The government believes that, when implemented appropriately, the broad-based black economic empowerment (BEE) strategy will ensure that every business operating in South Africa becomes both an implementer and a facilitator of economic transformation. The promotion and acceleration of broad-based BEE will be enhanced by the multiplier effect introduced by the various indirect BEE factors. Examples of these are preferential procurement and enterprise development.

When starting up your new business, it will be very important that you take BEE into account. This chapter will provide you with a broad understanding of black economic empowerment and, more importantly, will assist you in gaining the best possible business advantage when implementing the various requirements of BEE.

D A **black company** is one that is 50.1% owned by black persons and where there is substantial management control. Ownership refers to economic interest, while management refers to the membership of any board or similar governing body of the enterprise.

A **black empowered company** is one that is at least 25.1% owned by black persons and where there is substantial management control. Ownership refers to economic interests, while management refers to executive directors. This indicates whether black enterprise has control or not.

A **black woman-owned enterprise** is one with at least 25.1% representation of black women within the black equity and management portion.

A **community or broad-based enterprise** has an empowerment shareholder that represents a broad base of members such as a local community or where the benefits support a target group, such as black women, people living with disabilities, the youth, and workers. Shares are held through direct equity, non-profit organisations, and trusts.

A **cooperative or collective enterprise** is an autonomous association of people who voluntarily join together to meet their economic, social, and cultural needs and aspirations through the formation of a jointly owned enterprise and democratically controlled enterprise.

1. How will Jaque Khumalo, as a black woman, meet BEE requirements?

2. What are the advantages to Jaque's Treats of having a person of her profile as the business owner?

3. If Jaque needs an investment partner to provide capital for setting up her enterprise, what would you advise her in terms of choosing her partner and partnership structure?

4.3 The Black Economic Empowerment Act

The president signed the *Broad-Based Black Economic Empowerment Act, 53 of 2003* into law in January 2004. The objectives of the Act are to facilitate broad-based black economic empowerment by

* promoting economic transformation in order to enable meaningful participation of black people in the economy,

* achieving a substantial change in the racial composition of ownership and management structures and in the skilled occupations of existing and new enterprises,

* increasing the extent to which communities, workers, cooperatives, and other collective enterprises own and manage existing and new enterprises, and increasing their access to economic activities, infrastructure, and skills training,

* increasing the extent to which black women own and manage existing and new enterprises, and increasing their access to economic activities, infrastructure, and skills training,

* promoting investment programmes that lead to broad-based and meaningful participation in the economy by black people in order to achieve sustainable development and general prosperity,

* empowering rural and local communities by enabling access to economic activities, land, infrastructure, ownership, and skills, and

* promoting access to finance for black economic empowerment.

4.4 The Department of Trade and Industry

The Department of Trade and Industry (DTI) has been tasked with setting up, administrating, and implementing the black economic empowerment legislation. They have said that the Act and the Codes of Good Practice will promote the economic empowerment of all black people, including black women, black workers, black youth, black people with disabilities, and black people living in rural areas, through diverse but integrated socioeconomic strategies. These include

* increasing the number of black people who manage, own, and control enterprises and productive assets,

* facilitating ownership and management of enterprises and productive assets by communities, workers, cooperatives, and other collective enterprises,

* human resource and skills development,

* achieving equitable representation in all occupational categories and levels in the workforce,

* preferential procurement, and

* investment in enterprises that are owned or managed by black people.

4.5 The balanced BEE scorecard

In order to monitor the progress of the black economic empowerment legislation and the various strategies, the department has introduced what is referred to as a 'balanced scorecard' that will assess and measure the progress being made by enterprises and sectors in achieving BEE. The scorecard, as yet to be finalised and published by the department, will be used to rate a business or enterprise in the event that the sector has not introduced its own BEE charter and appropriate scorecard. The draft scorecard and explanations have been published under the heading 'BEE Codes of Good Practice'.

The generic DTI scorecard will measure three core elements of BEE:

* direct empowerment through ownership and control of enterprises and assets,
* human resource development and employment equity, and
* indirect empowerment through preferential procurement and enterprise development.

Government will use the total score to rank enterprises according to their progress in achieving broad-based BEE. The following are the categories for ranking:

* total score of 80% and above: excellent contributor to broad-based BEE,
* total score of 65% to 79.9%: good contributor to broad-based BEE,
* total score of 40% to 64.9%: satisfactory contributor to broad-based BEE,
* total score of 25% to 39%: limited contributor to broad-based BEE, and
* total score of below 25%: unsatisfactory contributor to broad-based BEE.

4.6 Measuring black economic empowerment

All BEE initiatives must be measurable, as this is critical in determining the progress made by businesses, sectors, and the economy as a whole towards the BEE objectives. There are seven key elements that are the pillars to broad-based BEE. These elements provide a common base for measuring the impact of BEE across different entities and sectors with the economy.

* **Ownership:** Ownership recognises and measures the entitlement of black people to the voting rights and economic interest associated with equity holding.
* **Management:** Management refers to the effective control of economic activities and resources. This involves the power to determine policies as well as the direction of economic activities and resources within a business.

* **Employment equity:** Employment equity is the promotion of equal opportunities through the elimination of unfair discrimination and through active measures to redress the disadvantages in employment experienced by black people.

* **Skills development:** Skills development refers to the development of core competencies of black people to facilitate their interaction in the mainstream of the economy.

* **Preferential procurement:** Preferential procurement is a measure designed to widen market access for entities in order to integrate them into the mainstream of the economy.

* **Enterprise development:** This aims to assist and accelerate the development of the operational and financial capacity of small and medium black owned and controlled entrepreneurial enterprises.

* **Residual or industry-specific factors:** Residual or industry-specific factors allow for other factors that may accelerate broad-based empowerment, and will include industry-specific initiatives as well as social development factors.

4.7 Industry-specific charters and scorecards

At the time of writing, the following industries and sectors had published their own BEE charters and scorecards.

* the construction industry ,
* the financial services sector,
* the forwarding and clearing sector,
* the information technology sector,
* the maritime industry,
* the mining industry,
* the petroleum sector, and
* the tourism industry.

When starting up your new business, make sure that you establish whether or nor your particular industry or sector has published a dedicated charter and scorecard. If not, you will be required to implement the generic or broad-based charter as provided by the Department of Trade and Industry.

4.8 Black economic empowerment rating agencies

The role of the rating agency is to assess, verify, and validate both the disclosed and the undisclosed BEE-related information of the business or enterprise.

This verification will be based on the principles contained in the broad-based BEE Codes of Good Practice or the relevant gazetted industry charters and scorecards.

Only rating agencies that are registered with the Department of Trade and Industry (DTI) and accredited by the South African National Accreditation System (SANAS) are recognised as legitimate.

4.8.1 BEE rating certificates

The BEE rating agency will provide business and enterprises with a BEE rating certificate after the evaluation. There is no specific requirement in terms of the nature of the certificate, but it must provide the following information:

* the name and identifiable physical location(s) of each site of the client's business or enterprise that has been BEE rated,
* the dates of granting BEE rating and validity,
* the expiry date of the rating certificate,
* a unique identification number,
* the standard and/or normative document including issue and/or revision used to evaluate the client,
* the name and/or mark/logo of the BEE rating agency,
* the scorecard against which the enterprise is being rated, and
* the BEE rating.

BEE rating certificates must show a banded total score in line with the range of BEE scores. The ranges of scores have been provided on page 44.

4.8.2 Request for a BEE rating

If you request for your business or enterprise to be rated, the agency will require that you personally be an authorised representative of the enterprise, and they will request that you provide the following information:

* the general features of the enterprise, including its name and the address(es) of its physical location(s),
* general information such as its activities, human and other resources, functions, and relationships in a larger corporation, if any, and
* information concerning the enterprise's use of consultancy relating to the implementation of BEE.

Before it agrees to go ahead with the rating, the agency must review your request. It has to ensure that

* the information is sufficient for conducting the review,
* the requirements for rating are clearly defined and documented and have been provided to the enterprise,
* any known difference in understanding between the BEE rating agency and the enterprise is resolved,
* the BEE rating agency has the competence and ability to perform the service, and
* the location and number of the applicant enterprise's operations, the time required to complete ratings, and any other points influencing activities or the rating process such as language, safety conditions, threats to impartiality, etc., are clarified and documented.

Based on this review, the agency will determine the skills it needs to include in its rating team.

It is obliged to maintain records of the justification for the decision.

After reviewing the request for rating, the BEE rating agency will notify the enterprise or business that it is accepting or not accepting the request for rating. The reasons for non-acceptance will be conveyed to the applicant (e.g., resource constraints).

4.8.3 Rating agreement

Before beginning the rating, an agreement must be established between the BEE rating agency and the enterprise or business, which

* requires the enterprise to supply any information needed for the intended rating, and
* requires the enterprise to conform to the requirements for BEE rating.

4.8.4 Rating evaluations

It is important to note that the BEE rating agency is required to have an established programme for carrying out periodic on-site evaluations at sufficiently close intervals to confirm the continued validity of the enterprise or business BEE rating. It is important to note as well that it is an ongoing process and not a once-off certification.

4.9 BEE and your new business

BEE, while legislated, is not enforced. However, it is in your best interests as a small business to comply wherever possible, as this will enhance your ability to do business with larger companies that need to maintain or improve their own scores, or if you wish to do business with government at any level.

We are now going to taker a closer look at BEE as it might apply to your business. It is important to note from the outset that, though the implementation of the BEE provisions is voluntary, it will become an economic imperative for most if not all businesses in South Africa. From today and well into the future, many aspects of doing business in South Africa will be governed by a company's or organisation's BEE credentials.

If you intend doing business with government, be it at national, provincial, and/or local level, you are going to have to ensure that you have a satisfactory, good, or preferably excellent BEE rating.

For example, if you are in the tourism industry and run an accommodation establishment and you are hoping to attract government officials to stay with you or use your facilities, you are going to have to provide them with confirmation of your BEE status before they will agree to make use of your establishment.

Evaluate your existing incoming business and clients, and potential new business for your company. How much more business could you generate if you had a favourable BEE rating?

We are now going to take a brief look at each of the BEE indicators and provide you with a few ideas and pointers that might be useful when planning your BEE strategy. Please note that these are by no means exhaustive and are only a few ideas for consideration.

4.9.1 Ownership

Ownership recognises and measures the entitlement of black people to the voting rights and economic interest associated with holding equity in a business.

In terms of ownership, it is more than probable that the BEE Codes of Good Practice, when published in their final format, will provide some form of exclusion for small business. Make sure that you establish the exact ownership requirements for your size of business and for your specific industry before setting up your BEE business plan.

A good example would be the Tourism Charter and Scorecard, which states that 'if a Tourism business is under the R5m turnover threshold, they will automatically be awarded 100% for ownership being 15% in 2009 and 20% in 2014'.

When deciding on what strategy to adopt in terms of ownership, make sure that you consider all of the options available to you. You should not only look at setting up an equity partnership but consider, for example, the merits of an employee shareholding.

Irrespective of the nature of the equity shareholding you intend implementing, make sure that you get professional advice on the exact legal requirements. Most banks or financial institutions will assist you in structuring the most appropriate scheme.

If you intend seeking an equity partner, make sure that the individual or organisation you intend bringing on board is in a position either to generate additional business or to add significant expertise that will benefit your new enterprise.

4.9.2 Management

> **Board representation** and **executive management** refer to the effective control of economic activities and resources. This involves the power to determine policies, as well as the direction of economic activities and resources.

Once again, there is every possibility that small business will be treated a little differently from big business. For example, owners and partners of small businesses will in all probability be deemed to be both board and executive managers of their enterprise. This is likely to occur when a small business does not have a board or executive structure.

By structuring your equity partnership (if you have chosen to engage equity partners) correctly from the outset, you will be able to ensure that you end up with a favourable score for Board Representation and Executive Management. Make sure that you take into account both the equity and management requirements before structuring your equity deal or partnership.

4.9.3 Employment equity

Employment equity is the promotion of equal opportunities through the elimination of unfair discrimination and action measures to redress the disadvantages in employment experienced by black people.

In the majority of BEE charters and scorecards, this is likely to take the form of

- black people as a percentage of management,
- black women as a percentage of management,
- black people as a percentage of supervisory/junior and skilled employees,
- black women as a percentage of supervisory/junior and skilled employees,
- black people as a percentage of total staff, and
- black women as a percentage of total staff.

When starting up a new business and when looking to engage employees, it would be wise to take the BEE requirements for employment equity into account right from the outset. This will enable you to maximise your rating without having to make significant changes to your employee structures.

If you yourself do not fall into a BEE category, as in the case of Jaque Khumalo, ensure that you engage employees who meet both the BEE requirements above and the various skills required for the business.

4.9.4 Skills development

Skills development refers to the development of core competencies of black people to facilitate their interaction in the mainstream of the economy.

In the majority of BEE charters and scorecards, this is likely to take the form of

- the percentage of your payroll spending on accredited training, including your contribution to the Skills Levy,
- the percentage of Skills Development Levy spending on black employees,
- the number of learnerships as a percentage of total employees, and
- the number of black learners as a percentage in proportion to total learners.

It would be wise for you to take the BEE skills development requirements into account before engaging employees for the new business. For example, you might consider taking on a learner from the outset. Call the Sector Education and Training Authority (SETA) responsible for your industry and ascertain the specific requirements for engaging a learner.

Look to building a training budget into your initial business plan. Call the Sector Education and Training Authority (SETA) responsible for your industry and ascertain what industry-specific training programmes are available, who runs them, and at what cost. As a small business owner, it is not always possible for you to set aside time to train your employees. By providing your employees with professional training from the outset, you will not only be supporting the BEE requirements but will be ensuring that your employees meet the appropriate skills levels required for the job.

4.9.5 Preferential procurement

D

> **Preferential procurement** is a measure designed to widen market access for entities in order to integrate them into the mainstream economy.

Essentially, preferential procurement means the total rands spent on purchases from BEE-compliant companies as a percentage of the total procurement spending of the business. The more you buy your supplies from BEE-compliant companies, the higher your own BEE rating will be in this regard.

In the majority of BEE charters and scorecards, this is likely to take the form of

- R1 for every R1 spent with Excellent (90%+) or Good (65%+ to 89%) BEE-compliant SMEs and black woman-owned BEE contributors.
- R0.50 for every R1 spent with Satisfactory (40%+ to 64%) BEE contributors.

Clearly, it will be very important for you to research your proposed suppliers carefully from the outset. Contact your industry association and ascertain whether or not a BEE supplier database exists. It is equally possible that a number of rating agencies will build supplier databases for various industries over the coming months and years. Your particular industry may have formed a BEE council, and they in turn would in all probability research and compile an industry-specific procurement database.

It should not be difficult for you to score well in terms of the procurement requirement, but it will undoubtedly involve an investment in time and research. Remember that those doing business with you will also be seeking an excellent or good BEE rating in order to build their own scores.

4.9.6 Enterprise development

Enterprise development aims to assist and accelerate the development of the operational and financial capacity of small and medium black owned and controlled entrepreneurial enterprises.

Contributions to enterprise development, whether by spending money or management time, relate solely to initiatives targeted for the benefit of black-owned companies. You should note that only assistance to black-owned and black-empowered SMMEs is likely to qualify in this indicator.

Initiatives that will be considered in enterprise development are likely to include the support and funding provided to black-owned and black-empowered SMMEs, as well as various business linkage initiatives that provide business opportunities to these enterprises.

Essentially, you will first need to identify a particular black-owned/black-empowered SMME, or more than one of these, and consider a number of ways in which you or your business can assist them. Assistance and guidance could take many forms, some of which may involve advertising, training, procurement, cost-saving information, and operational expertise.

4.9.7 Residual factors

'Residual factors' is an item that allows for other factors that may accelerate broad-based empowerment. Residual factors will include industry-specific initiatives as well as social development factors.

Generally speaking, residual factors will involve your participation, either through time or money, with organisations likely to be outside of your specific industry, or with black-owned businesses linked to your specific industry. Assisting your local community in some way or another and or supporting and guiding a small supplier would be deemed to be a residual factor.

Corporate social investment initiatives, whether they made are in time or money, involving health, education, poverty alleviation, and community development are all excellent examples of the types of initiative you should consider.

4.9.8 The BEE scorecard

The scorecard looks as follows:

Core components	BEE elements	Weighting	Indicators	Indicator weighting	Targets	Sub-minimum	Bonus/preferential weighting provisions
Direct empowerment	Ownership (code ref BEE 100)	20%	Unrestricted voting rights in the enterprise in the hands of black people	3%	25% + 1 vote		Introduction of new entrants and BEE ownership in excess of target
			Unrestricted voting rights in the enterprise in the hands of black women	2%	10%		
			Economic interest in the enterprise to which black people are entitled	4%	25%		
			Economic interest in the enterprise to which black women are entitled	2%	10%		
			Economic interest in the enterprise to which black designated groups are entitled	1%	2.5%		
			Level of unrestricted entitlement of black people to receive their economic interest in the enterprise (as percentage of total ownership)	8%	25%		
	Management (ref BEE 200)	10%	Weighted management representation scorecard	10%	40%		Women management. Different management positions weighed according to seniority and executive involvement

Core components	BEE elements	Weighting	Indicators	Indicator weighting	Targets	Sub-minimum	Bonus/preferential weighting provisions
Human resources development	Employment Equity (ref BEE 300)	10%	Weighted employment equity scorecard	10%	50%		Women representation
	Skills Development (ref BEE 400)	20%	Investment in skills development (in addition to Skills Development Levy) as a percentage of payroll	15%	3%		Fast-track programmes for Black employees and management. Provision of skills development programmes and Learnerships in priority skill areas
			Learnership positions (as a percentage of employees)	5%	3%		
Indirect empowerment	Preferential procurement (ref BEE 500)	20%	Affirmative procurement from excellent BEE companies (80–100 points)	18%	50%		Procurement from excellent contributors (recognised at R1.25 of every R1 spend) Procurement from good contributors (recognised at R1 of every R1 spend)
			Affirmative procurement from good BEE companies (80–100 points)				
			Affirmative procurement from satisfactory BEE companies (80–100 points)				
			Implementation of robust independent verification and reporting mechanisms to avoid fronting	2%	Mechanism which verifies status of suppliers		Procurement from satisfactory contributors (recognised at 50c of every R1 spend)
		Enterprise development (ref BEE 600)	Monetary investment in SMME with excellent or good BEE score	8%	35–10% (depending on base used)		The percentage scores achieved through monetary investment and quantifiable non-monetary support are summed to arrive at the enterprise development points (max achievable is 10)
			Quantitative non-monetary support to SMME with excellent or good BEE rating	2%	2–5% (dep ending on base used)		

Core components	BEE elements	Weighting	Indicators	Indicator weighting	Targets	Sub-minimum	Bonus/preferential weighting provisions
	Residual element		Industry-specific initiatives to facilitate the inclusion of black people in the sector (as a percentage of net profit)	10%	3%		Total contribution towards these initiatives is summed relative to net profit of an enterprise. The total achievable percentage score is 10. Initiatives that do not promote empowerment of black people are specifically excluded
			Industry-specific initiatives to promote black economic empowerment (as a percentage of net profit)				
			Corporate social investment initiatives in health, education, poverty alleviation, and community develop-ment (as a percentage of net profit)				
Total	Element weighting	100%	Indicator weighting	100%		Sub-minimum	

4.10 Self-evaluation

1. Locate at least three BEE rating agencies and compare their fees and services. Keep this on file should you wish to be rated for your BEE score.

2. Name three advantages of being a BEE-compliant and rated enterprise.

3. What is the difference between black economic empowerment and employment equity?

4. In your own words, explain the concept of preferential procurement.

5. Which industries already have specific BEE charters in place?

Forms of business

5.1 Learning outcomes

After you have studied this chapter, you should be able to

- identify a suitable form of business for your small enterprise, and
- compare the statutory requirements of the various forms of business.

5.2 Introduction

This chapter introduces the various options that an entrepreneur can choose from when establishing a small business. The recommendation, however, is that you should look to keeping it as simple as possible. As a small business, it is recommended that you initially consider forming either a sole proprietorship or a partnership.

A lot of people believe that they should register at least as a close corporation, if not a company, in order to start up a business. This is not correct. The reason why a close corporation is provided is essentially to relieve businesses of the complex requirements and formalities of the *Companies Act* while allowing them corporate status and a legal identity distinct from their members. A close corporation has a legal personality (which means it can act in its own name) with all the benefits this involves.

However, as a small business owner, you may not need to go to the trouble of registering and setting up a close corporation. When starting up your new business – and especially if you are on your own or plan to have one or two partners – it is recommended that you consider a sole proprietorship or a partnership.

Jaque will have to look closely at her business requirements and her possible business partners and family members to decide what the best form of enterprise for Jaque's Treats will be. She will have to consider a number of possibilities and weigh up the advantages and disadvantages of each before deciding on the most appropriate type of business. No single form may fit exactly, but the best fit is the one she will be trying to determine.

This chapter will take you through the requirements of each entity and, on the basis of the advantages and disadvantages, you should decide which entity suits your needs the best.

5.3 Forms of enterprise for a business

As an entrepreneur, you must decide which form of business is the most suitable for your needs. As shown in the diagram below, an entrepreneur can choose from any one of four forms of enterprise:

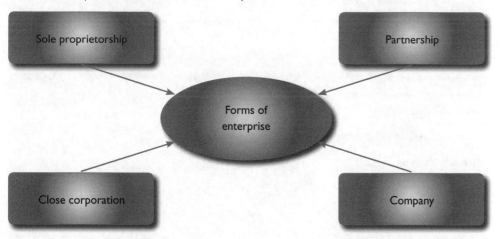

The following table may assist you in deciding the best form of business for your situation. The most appropriate forms of business are marked against each of the scenarios. Keep in mind that it is impossible to list all possible scenarios, and that your choice can very easily be influenced by more than one factor. This table is only a guide. If you are unsure as to what to do, make sure you consult an expert.

Consideration	Sole trader	Partnership	Close corporation	Company
If you are in business on your own, for yourself, without major expansion plans	X		X	
If you have partners		X	X	X
If you know your partner(s) well and trust them, and if the business is simple with not too many assets over which dispute can arise		X		
Partners with a short-term business in mind		X		
If some of your partners are not people but organisations				X
If you want to sell the business one day			X	X
If shareholding is (or will become) more complex than a simple 50/50 or 60/40 split.			X	X
If you will be running a really low-risk business	X	X		
If the business risk is slightly higher			X	X
If you want to tender for government contracts			X	X
If you are working on an absolute shoe-string budget	X	X		
If you have some resources to start with but need to keep costs very low			X	
If you have a fair amount of financial resources				X
If you don't have to convey an impression of being a substantial business	X	X	X	
If you have to convey the impression that you have a substantial business				X

Factors to be considered when choosing a suitable form of enterprise include

- the need to involve third parties from a financial point of view (How great are the financial needs of your business? Are these high and will you be looking for investors?),
- legal requirements in respect of establishing the enterprise and complying with regulations,
- the expected ability of the enterprise to exist independently of its owners (that is, for how long is the business likely to operate?),
- the liability of the owners of the enterprise for debts and their share of the profits (in some cases, the owner's assets are at risk if the enterprise should fail),
- the continuity of the enterprise, including the extent of direct control, and
- the tax position of the various forms of enterprise and how this will affect the owners.

Note the following questions that you and other entrepreneurs must ask yourselves before you choose an enterprise:

- Do I want to involve another person or persons in the enterprise?
- What are the legal requirements and regulations that must be met when starting an enterprise?
- Must the enterprise be able to exist independently of its owners?
- Do I want to be liable for the debts of the enterprise, and how must the profits be allocated?
- If I die, should the enterprise continue, and how will it function?
- What will my tax situation be?

5.4 Formation procedures for businesses

Different business entities have different statutory requirements regulating their formation and registration. All South African companies are governed by the *Companies Act*. The Act prescribes the procedures to be followed to form a private or public company. Close corporations are governed by the *Close Corporations Act*. There are no formal procedures relating to the formation of a partnership or sole proprietorship.

5.5 Sole proprietorship

A **sole proprietorship** is an enterprise that belongs to only one person and therefore has no partners or co-owners. The owner can appoint people to work for him or her. He or she provides the capital, takes all the decisions alone, manages the enterprise, and accepts all the responsibility for profits and debts. The lifetime of the enterprise is linked to that of the owner, and there is unlikely to be a difference between private and business property.

There are no formal requirements for the establishment and the auditing of a sole proprietorship, other than the need to register for income tax purposes, for VAT purposes if applicable, and to register your employees for unemployment insurance and workmen's compensation. These topics are all covered in other chapters of this book.

Advantages

The following are the advantages of a sole proprietorship:

- From a legal point of view, it is easy to start and to close down a sole proprietorship.
- All income belongs to the owner.
- The functioning of the enterprise is simple and can easily be adapted to changing circumstances.
- Accounting requirements are basic and do not require auditing.
- The owner takes and makes all of the business decisions and is not required to obtain the agreement of others before implementation.

Disadvantages

Disadvantages of a sole proprietorship are as follows:

- The creditworthiness of the enterprise is limited to the assets of the owner.
- The owner is fully responsible for losses and can lose his or her private possessions if the enterprise is unable to meet its debt obligations.
- There is uncertainty regarding the continued existence of the business if the owner dies.
- If it is sold or taken over, the enterprise will no longer exist. It must therefore be re-founded legally from scratch.

- The future of the enterprise is limited, not only in terms of its establishment, but also in terms of expansion. A sole proprietorship can only develop to a level where it meets the owner's capital ability. If more capital is to be secured, it could mean changing the form of the enterprise in order to raise the required finance.

5.6 Partnership

A **partnership** is formed when a group of people get together and combine their capital, labour, know-how, and experience in the form of an agreement with the aim of starting up a business.

The *Companies Act* limits the membership in a partnership to 20 persons (who may be either natural or juristic persons), except for partnerships in certain recognised professions which include accountants and attorneys.

No other statutory provisions, such as auditing requirements, govern partnerships, but they are subject to the general principles of the law of contract and to various special principles of common law applicable particularly to partnerships. They are not separate legal entities, and no registration formalities are required.

A partnership is formed when at least two and not more than 20 people conclude an agreement. This contract, which should preferably be drawn up by an attorney, contains the names of the partners, the name and nature of the enterprise, the contributions (financial or otherwise) of the partners, remuneration of the partners, division of profits, and other aspects. Partners should be chosen carefully, and partnership agreements should be drawn up by an attorney.

Advantages

The following are the advantages of a partnership:

- The management skills, personal expertise, decision-making abilities, and special characteristics of a number of people are pooled.
- Opportunities for obtaining capital are usually more favourable, and each partner can contribute to the capital of the enterprise.
- The legal requirements, such as a partnership agreement, can be easily dealt with by an attorney

- In a partnership, the partners are taxed in their personal capacity and not collectively. The profit is shared, and each partner's share is taxed separately.

- Accounting requirements are basic and do not require auditing.

Disadvantages

Disadvantages of a partnership are as follows:

- It is not always easy to find suitable and trustworthy partners with the appropriate skills and talents required for the business.

- Partners are jointly liable for the debts that other partners may incur in the enterprise. Trust between partners will be essential.

- Each partner is both a principal and an agent of the business and can commit the other partner(s) through his or her actions, for example by incurring debts.

- The partnership can be dissolved by any change in its composition, and the life expectancy of a partnership is therefore always uncertain.

5.7 Close corporation

Since the *Close Corporations Act, 69 of 1984* was promulgated in June 1984, the close corporation (CC) has become a popular form of business entity. The main objective of the *Close Corporations Act* was to relieve businesses from the complex requirements and formalities of the *Companies Act*, while allowing them corporate status and a legal identity distinct from their members.

A close corporation is formed by filing a founding statement with the Companies and Intellectual Property Registration Office of South Africa (CIPRO). Private companies with qualifying members can be converted into close corporations and close corporations may be converted into private companies. A close corporation indicates its status by the letters 'CC' or the words 'Close Corporation' at the end of its name, and the word 'company' may not appear in the name. The close corporation's name, its registration number, and the names of the members must appear on all business documents.

A close corporation does not have shareholders, only members who all have an interest in the business. This interest is expressed as a percentage of all the interests in the corporation. The total interest must be 100% at all times. Instead of having share capital, close corporations have members' interests, the distribution of which is arrived at by agreement with the other members.

At the time of founding the close corporation, each member must make a contribution either in the form of money, movable or fixed assets, or services rendered, or by purchasing an interest from an existing member. The extent of a member's interest does not have to be in proportion to that member's contribution. Unless otherwise agreed in an association agreement between the members, a sale of a member's interest requires the consent of all of the other members, failing which the member can sell his or her interest back to the close corporation.

Close corporations may provide financial assistance for the acquisition of members' interests and may themselves acquire members' interests from any member. However, if the close corporation does not remain both solvent and liquid immediately after giving that assistance or acquiring that interest, the members will have personal liability to creditors prejudiced as a result.

A close corporation may be formed by at least one but not more than 10 members. The only persons qualified to become members are

- natural persons, including non-residents (a juristic person such as a company may not directly or indirectly hold an interest in a close corporation),

- a trustee of a testamentary trust (a trustee of an *inter vivo* trust – a trust created by contract – is specifically excluded from membership), and

- a trustee, administrator, executor, or curator for a member who is insolvent, deceased, mentally disordered, or otherwise incapable of managing his or her affairs.

Natural persons may not hold members' interests as nominees for persons who are disqualified from being members. Companies, partnerships, societies, and clubs are therefore excluded. Close corporations are managed by their members. There is no separate board of directors or management body, and each member is entitled to participate in the management unless the members agree to the contrary.

Each member stands in a fiduciary relationship to the corporation and may become liable to the corporation for losses suffered as a result of breach of fiduciary duties. The members may enter into an association agreement to govern their relationship. However, if no such agreement is concluded, the *Close Corporations Act* contains provisions regulating the relationship of members.

D Fiduciary means acting in good faith to safeguard the interests of a person or an entity. An executor or a custodian, for instance, plays a fiduciary role.

The close corporation is largely self-regulating. Relatively few provisions of the *Close Corporations Act* are linked to criminal sanctions. Instead, members may lose their limited liability status if they transgress certain provisions of the Act.

Advantages

The advantages of a close corporation are as follows:

- The legal requirements are relatively simple and easy to comply with.
- The close corporation has a simple management structure and most decisions are taken informally by the members.
- All members are part of the management and have a direct interest in the success of the business.
- The close corporation has a legal personality (it can act in its own name) with all the benefits this involves. This gives the enterprise continuity.
- The members are not taxed personally for the dividends they receive.
- An auditor does not have to be appointed, only an accounting officer.
- Annual general meetings are not mandatory.
- Any addendum to the original founding document can be added simply by registering the addendum.

Disadvantages

The following are disadvantages of a close corporation:

- The fact that a close corporation may have only 10 members can have a restricting effect on the enterprise if it wishes to expand.
- The close corporation can experience fundraising difficulties as the members have limited liability for the debts of the corporation. This makes it difficult to obtain credit.
- If a member wishes to sell his or her interest, all the other members of the corporation must give their consent.

5.7.1 Registration of close corporations

A CC name must be reserved with and approved by the Companies and Intellectual Property Registration Office of South Africa (CIPRO).

> It is advisable to suggest alternative names in case the first name is deemed unsuitable by CIPRO.

Registration of a close corporation (CC) is then a relatively simple and quick process. The only constitutional document required is a founding statement, which must be filed with CIPRO.

The full process is covered in chapter 7, 'Register to operate'.

5.7.2 Statutory accounting and auditing requirements for close corporations

The requirements relating to the maintenance of accounting records are similar to those for a company. A CC's annual financial statements must be drafted within nine months after its year-end. The annual financial statements must be approved and signed by or on behalf of members who hold at least 51% of the members' interest and must consist of

- a balance sheet and notes,
- an income statement or any similar financial statement, and
- a members' net investment statement.

The financial statements must fairly present the state of affairs and the result of the operations of the business in accordance with Generally Accepted Accounting Practice (GAAP).

Close corporations are not subject to a compulsory audit. However, the close corporation is required to appoint an independent accounting officer, who is responsible for the preparation of the financial statements and who must be a member of one of the recognised professional accounting bodies. Under the *Close Corporations Act*, an accounting officer is required to ensure that the annual financial statements are in agreement with the books and records of the close corporation.

The disclosure requirements for a close corporation are subject to the overriding requirement of fair presentation. The complexity of the financial statements would depend on the needs of the members, who, as owners and managers of the close corporation, are the primary recipients of the financial information.

5.8 Companies

As it is most unlikely that a small business will seek to form and register a company from the outset, the information contained below gives only a broad summary of the statutory requirements. Should you be looking to form a company, it is suggested that you seek professional assistance or guidance.

> A **company** is a legal person in its own right. In other words, it has a 'life' independent or separate from that of the shareholders. There are various kinds of company:
>
> • private company,
>
> • public company, and
>
> • company limited by guarantee (such a company does not issue shares and is not profit orientated).

The *Companies Act, 61 of 1973* makes provision for two types of company, namely

• a company having share capital, which can be either a public company or a private company, and

• a company that has no share capital (this company is also referred to as a company limited by guarantee).

5.8.1 Limited liability company

The most common form of business entity in South Africa is the limited liability company. Companies can be limited by guarantee or limited by shares. Companies limited by guarantee are generally 'not-for-profit' organisations that primarily promote religious, charitable, educational, or other similar interests.

The names of companies limited by guarantee must end with the word 'Limited' (short for 'Limited by Guarantee'). Companies having share capital may be public or private companies. The names of public companies end with the word 'Limited', whereas those of private companies must end with the words '(Proprietary) Limited'.

A private company is one which, by its articles,

- restricts the right to transfer its shares,
- limits the number of its members to 50, and
- prohibits any offer for the subscription of any shares or debentures to the public.

All other companies are public companies and, as such, are not subject to the above restrictions. A public company may be listed or unlisted. Listed companies are subject to the rules and regulations laid down by the Johannesburg Securities Exchange South Africa (JSE).

Listed means that a company is accepted and registered to have its shares traded publicly on a stock market, such as the JSE in South Africa.

For a private company, the minimum number of shareholders and directors is one, while a public company must have at least seven shareholders (unless it is a wholly owned subsidiary of another company) and two directors. Directors need not own shares in the company, and need not be resident in South Africa, but a South African resident must be appointed as a public officer of the company to handle income tax matters. The company secretary of a public company must be a South African resident. The board of directors is responsible for the daily management of the company for the benefit of its shareholders, and acts for the company in transactions entered into by it. The shareholders exercise their powers in general meetings. The annual general meeting must be held within nine months of the financial year-end and not more than 15 months after the last such meeting. Shareholders may be individuals or corporate bodies, and any or all of the company's shares may be held by non-residents.

Shares can be in any denomination, and no-par-value shares are permitted. There is no minimum amount of share capital required (other than the requirement that on subscription each subscriber must subscribe for at least one share), nor is there any prescribed ratio between share capital and borrowings.

A **no-par-value share** is a share that has no stated value (or par value) when it is first issued for sale.

A private company, with a maximum of 50 shareholders, must be registered with the Companies and Intellectual Property Registration Office of South Africa (CIPRO) and is identified by the words '(Proprietary) Limited' after its name. The company may commence operations only after registration with CIPRO, to which it pays an annual levy.

A private company is required by law to prepare audited financial statements annually. Appointing a chartered accountant is therefore mandatory. The company may be established by either an attorney or a chartered accountant. All prescriptions relating to authority, liability, management, the sale of shares, remuneration, or dividends, are indicated in the company's memorandum and articles of association. The chartered accountant or attorney assists by ensuring that annual tax returns and so on are submitted. Directors can be prosecuted if legal requirements are not strictly met.

The principle that a company is a separate entity and exists separately from its shareholders applies to both private and public companies. A company can enter into contracts and can sue or be sued in its own name. A shareholder's liability for the debts of the company is limited to the amount of capital invested in shares. Partly paid shares are not permitted. A director may be held liable to indemnify the company or its shareholders against losses suffered by them in the following circumstances:

- unauthorised loans to directors or companies controlled by directors,
- breach of trust or faith, or wrongs committed, by the director,
- reckless trading or fraud,
- untrue statements contained in a prospectus, and
- failure to repay monies received in respect of a share offer within a specified period.

A **prospectus** is the publicising by a company of a new listing of shares. It describes them and invites the public to buy them.

Private companies may not offer shares to the public. 'The public' is widely construed. Offers of shares to the public by public companies are controlled by statutory restrictions.

Prior to the *Companies Amendment Act, 37 of 1999*, a company was not entitled to provide any financial assistance to any person (other than an employee) in connection with the purchase of or subscription for its shares, and a company could not purchase its own shares. The amendment allows a company to reduce its capital by acquiring its own shares. A subsidiary company is entitled to acquire shares and be a shareholder in its holding company to a maximum of 10% of the issued share capital of the holding company. Such acquisition is, however, subject to liquidity and solvency provisions protecting the creditors of the companies.

Advantages

The advantages of a company are as follows:

- The company is a legal person in its own right and therefore exists independently from its shareholders. In this way, some of the disadvantages of a sole proprietorship and a partnership are overcome.
- Its shareholders have limited liability for debts that it incurs.
- Shares, and therefore ownership, can be transferred.
- The private company is free from many of the formalities required of a public company.
- The company and its members are taxed separately.

Disadvantages

The following are disadvantages of a company:

- Various extra costs must be met, such as the founding costs, annual subscriptions, and the cost of issuing shares.
- There are extensive prescriptions for establishing and managing the company.
- As a result of the compulsory publication of its statements, constitution, and so on, the company is known to everyone, including its competitors.

5.8.2 External company and branch operations

Instead of operating through a South African subsidiary, a foreign company may operate through a branch in South Africa. A company incorporated outside South Africa that establishes a place of business in South Africa is classified as an 'external company'. The definition of an external company has been extended to deem a foreign company, which acquires immovable property in South Africa, to have established a place of business in South Africa. An 'external company' is obliged to register with CIPRO and must comply with the provisions of the *Companies Act*. These include the submission of statutory returns and the filing of annual financial statements for its entire operations (and not only its South African operations) with CIPRO, where they are open to public scrutiny. Exemption from the obligation to file those accounts can be applied for and is fairly readily granted.

The 'external' company is required to appoint a South African resident who is authorised to accept notices served on the company. Once registered, the 'external' company will effectively be treated under South African law like a South African incorporated company; for example, it may be sued in South Africa.

5.8.3 Unlimited liability companies

Members of certain organised professions, such as attorneys, medical practitioners, and accountants, are allowed to incorporate. Their companies are private companies but do not confer limited liability on the members, who are jointly and severally liable for the debts of the company. These companies are identified by the word 'Incorporated' at the end of their names instead of '(Proprietary) Limited'.

5.8.4 Registration of companies

Incorporation of a company entails the following steps:

- reserving a company name,
- filing the memorandum and articles, and
- filing the written consent of auditors to act for the company.

A company name must be reserved with and approved by CIPRO.

It is advisable to suggest alternative names in case the first name is deemed unsuitable by CIPRO.

The memorandum and articles must also be filed with CIPRO and then completed in the form prescribed in the *Companies Act*. Both documents have to be signed by each subscriber to the memorandum. The persons signing the memorandum and the articles must state their full name, occupation, and residential, business, and postal addresses.

The memorandum of a company is the document that deals with the external structure of the company. The memorandum must state the purpose for which the company is formed; it must describe the main business that the company will conduct. The memorandum must also indicate, among other things,

- the name of the company,
- the company's main object, although there may be any number of ancillary objects, and
- the amount of authorised share capital (not all of which is required to be issued).

There is no minimum capital requirement.

The articles of association determine the internal structure of the company. Schedule 1 of the *Companies Act* contains an example of articles for a public company in Table A, and for a private company in Table B. However, a company is not compelled to follow one of those examples when drafting its articles. The *Companies Act* prescribes the content of the memorandum, but not the articles. The only requirement is that the articles do not conflict with the law or with the provisions of the *Companies Act*.

A company is not allowed to commence business until CIPRO issues a certificate that entitles the company to do so.

5.8.5 Shareholders and directors

For a private company, the minimum number of shareholders and directors is one (the sole shareholder may also be the sole director), while a public company must have at least seven shareholders (unless it is a wholly owned subsidiary of another company) and two directors. No residence or nationality restrictions apply to either shareholders or directors.

5.8.6 Statutory auditing requirements for companies

Accounting principles

Statements of Generally Accepted Accounting Practice (GAAP) are drafted by the South African Institute of Chartered Accountants and, after a period of publication for comment, approved by the Accounting Practices Board (APB). The APB consists of representatives from the accounting profession, commerce, and industry.

Statements of GAAP must be followed in the preparation of the financial statements of companies subject to the *Companies Act*. They are also relevant to the financial statements of other entities purporting to achieve fair presentation.

Form and content of financial statements

The *Companies Act* does not require a company to specify how its net profit for the year is made up, but does require certain items of income and expenditure to be detailed, such as turnover, depreciation, directors' remuneration, interest paid, and provision for taxation. If a company or group is involved in more than one type of business, the directors' report must indicate the proportion of profit attributable to each type of business. Notes to the financial statements usually provide details of all significant items shown on the balance sheet.

In addition to the *Companies Act* requirements, GAAP requires the disclosure of information concerning the company's accounting policies, details of taxation, extraordinary items, prior-year adjustments in the income statement, and other matters. Additional disclosure requirements apply to companies listed on the JSE. These requirements call for the disclosure of directors' interests in the share capital of the company, employees' share incentive schemes, and borrowing powers. They also require interim and preliminary reports to the members. The Second King Report on Corporate Governance has also recommended disclosure of directors' remuneration and benefits on an individual basis.

Accounting records

In terms of the *Companies Act*, all companies must keep accounting records in one of the 11 official languages. At a minimum, these records must include

- the assets and liabilities of the company,
- a fixed-assets register,
- cash receipts and payments,
- details of goods purchased and sold, and
- annual stocktaking (inventory) statements.

The accounting records must fairly present the state of affairs and business of the company and explain the transactions and financial position of the trade or business of the company.

Annual financial statements

In terms of the *Companies Act*, the directors of every company must prepare annual financial statements and present them to the annual general meeting of the company. At a minimum, the annual financial statements must consist of

- a balance sheet and notes,
- an income statement and notes,
- a directors' report,
- an auditors' report, and
- a cash flow statement.

The annual financial statements must fairly present the state of affairs of the company as at the financial year-end and its profit or loss for that year in conformity with Generally Accepted Accounting Practice (GAAP). If a company has subsidiaries at the end of its financial year and is not a wholly owned subsidiary of another company incorporated in South Africa, it has an obligation to prepare group financial statements. These must, in the same way as the company's own financial statements, fairly present the position and results of the group and must also conform to GAAP. Both the company and group financial statements must set out certain additional information prescribed by the *Companies Act*, must be approved by the directors, and must be signed by two directors or, if there is only one director, by that director.

Interim reports

Public companies and branches of foreign companies (external companies) are required to send all members and debenture holders a half-yearly interim report, fairly presenting the business and operations of the company (or, if applicable, the group). It is not required that such interim reports be audited, but they must be approved by the directors and signed on their behalf by two of the directors. Private companies are not required to provide an interim report to members.

Provisional financial statements

If a public company has not issued annual financial statements within three months after its year-end, it must (within such three-month period) issue provisional financial statements to its members and debenture holders. These must fairly present the business and operations of the company or, if applicable, the group.

The requirements for private companies are less stringent. If a private company has not issued its financial statements within six months after its year-end, CIPRO may, on application by a member and for good cause shown, require that provisional financial statements be submitted to that member. It is not necessary that such provisional annual financial statements be audited, but they must be approved and signed by the company's directors.

Annual audit requirement

The financial statements of both public and private companies are subject, under the *Companies Act*, to an annual audit. Only chartered accountants registered with the Public Accountants and Auditors Board may be appointed as auditors for the purposes of the annual audit.

Filing and disclosure requirements

Copies of a company's annual financial statements and group annual financial statements (if any) must be sent to the shareholders and debenture holders of the company not less than 21 days before the date of the company's annual general meeting. Public companies and external companies are required to file a copy of their annual financial statements with CIPRO within six months from the end of their financial year. Private companies are not required to do so, although the Second King Report on Corporate Governance has recommended that the *Companies Act* be amended to require this. In the case of an external company, it must also file a copy of its annual financial statements as prepared in terms of the requirements of the jurisdiction in which it is incorporated. External companies can apply for exemption from this and other requirements, and such exemption is fairly readily granted.

5.9 Business trusts

A business trust is a trust where the trust deed (the document in terms of which the trust is created) authorises the trustees (the persons who administer the trust) to carry on a business for the benefit of the beneficiaries identified in the trust deed. The purpose of this entity is to carry on the business and to distribute the profits among the beneficiaries. The trustees manage the business on behalf of the trust. They only have those management powers that are given to them in terms of the trust deed.

5.10 Taxation on business entities

The effect or impact of income taxation often determines the choice of the most suitable business in many cases. The taxation policy changes frequently; for example, when the Minister of Finance announces certain tax increases or concessions in the budget speech each year, or when the South African Revenue Service (SARS) makes amendments to existing legislation. Such changes have specific tax implications and it is therefore important for the business owners to know how the tax policy affects them.

A close corporation and a company possess their own legal personality, which is not the case with a sole proprietor or a partnership. This means that the persons in a sole proprietorship and the persons in a partnership are usually responsible for tax, debt obligations, and the commitments of the business. This is termed 'unlimited liability'. The shareholders of companies and members of close corporations have what is termed 'limited liability' in respect of the commitments of the particular business form. The person can therefore be held responsible to a limited extent for the commitments of the company or close corporation.

The following table provides a comparison of different business structures

Business structure					
	Sole proprietorship	Partnership	Close corporation	Company	Business trust
Number of members or shareholders and directors	One – the owner.	Two to 20 partners.	One to 10 members. Does not need separate board of directors.	One to 50 shareholders. Minimum one for private company, seven for public company. Minimum one director for private company, two for public company.	Number of members depends on the trust deed. Trustees limited to 20.
Capital contributions	Limited to the contribution of the owner.	Limited to the contribution of the separate partners.	Limited to the contribution of the members.	Limited to the contribution of the founders.	Limited to the contribution of the founders.

Business structure					
	Sole proprietorship	Partnership	Close corporation	Company	Business trust
Formation	Simple. No formal requirements.	Simple. Partnership agreement recommended.	A founding statement should be registered and a certificate of incorporation issued.	Memorandum and articles of association are registered and certificate of incorporation is issued.	An agreement between the founder and trustee for the benefit of the trustee is necessary. The Master of the Supreme Court must give authority to the trustee.
Legal personality	The business is not a separate legal entity.	The business is not a separate legal entity.	The business is a separate legal entity.	The business is a separate legal entity.	The business is regarded as a legal entity for some purposes (e.g. tax and VAT), but in terms of the common law it is not regarded as a separate legal entity.
Liability Distribution of profits	Unlimited. The profits belong to the owner.	Unlimited. Partnership agreement stipulates the distribution of profits.	Limited. Resolution should be passed approving distribution or it should have been validated by the association agreement.	Limited. Shareholders become entitled to a share of the net profit when dividends are declared.	Depends on the situation. The trust deed states how net profit should be dealt with.
Taxpayer	The business is not a separate taxpayer. The owner includes income from the business in his or her own gross income.	The business is not a separate taxpayer. Partners include profit share from the business in their own gross income.	The business is a separate taxpayer.	The business is a separate taxpayer.	The business is a separate taxpayer.

Business structure					
	Sole proprietorship	Partnership	Close corporation	Company	Business trust
Tax losses	Losses from the business can be offset against any other income.	Each partner's share of losses from the business can be offset against his or her other income.	Losses retained within the close corporation cannot be offset against members' other income.	Losses retained within the company cannot be offset against shareholders' other income	Losses are retained in the trust, where they may be carried forward to the next year, to be set off against the income of the trust in that year (and succeeding years).
Audit	Not required by law.	Not required by law.	Not required by law. The appointed accounting officer performs an accounting review.	An independent audit of the financial statements by a registered auditor is required by law.	Not required by law.

Source: Provided by and adapted from, Adv. M Moolman

5.11 Self-evaluation

1. What is the maximum number of members that each of the following forms of enterprise may have? Write your answers in the table next to each form of enterprise.

Form of enterprise	Maximum members
Sole proprietorship	
Partnership	
Close corporation	
Private company	

2. Name three disadvantages of a sole proprietorship.

3. Abdul Parker, Johan Roux, and Masiya Skozana decided to start a consultation enterprise for engineers, Apex Engineering Consultants. It would cost R65 000 to get the enterprise going. Abdul contributed R26 000, while Johan contributed R13 000, and Masiya contributed R19 500. To find the

remaining R6 500, they asked Andrew Malherbe (who has his own enterprise) to invest the amount in Apex Engineering Consultants in exchange for 10% interest in the enterprise.

(a) What form of enterprise will be the most suitable for Apex Engineering Consultants? Give two reasons for your answer.

(b) Indicate each person's contribution to the enterprise and his interest in it.

Member	Contribution of interest	Percentage
Abdul		
Johan		
Masiya		
Andrew	R6 500	10%
Total	R65 000	100%

4. In what circumstances would you consider starting a private company?

5. Why would you follow Standards of Generally Accepted Accounting Practices in your enterprise?

6. What form of enterprise would you recommend for Jaque's Treats? Give three reasons for your answer.

7. Solly and Bongani, two old friends from school, have decided to go into business together. They both did very well in carpentry and woodwork, and have decided to establish a furniture-making business called Two Carpenters. They each have some tools, but they need to invest in larger equipment and machinery and find premises where they have enough space for their work. They also need to invest in good quality timber to begin producing furniture items, and will employ a few unskilled workers whom they can train to assist them in cutting, assembling, and finishing their pieces.

(a) What form of business would you recommend for Two Carpenters?

(b) What are the risks to Solly and Bongani for this form of business?

(c) What registration process should they follow?

(d) What are the financial and auditing requirements for such a business?

6 Property and premises

6.1 Learning outcomes

After you have studied this chapter you should be able to

- ensure that your business premise is correctly zoned for your enterprise,

- meet legal requirements for signage, road access, water usage and environmental aspects for your business premises,

- meet building regulations on your premises,

- ensure that your business premises have appropriate fire-fighting, detection, and alarm systems in place, and

- obtain a fire clearance certificate.

6.2 Introduction

There are certain legal matters that you will need to take into account when building, buying, or renting a property for the purposes of running your business. These legal requirements may cover such matters as the zoning of the property for commercial use, freedom from a land claim, compliance with environmental laws, design of the building to incorporate building codes, industry- or business-specific health and safety requirements, and so on. A visit to the local municipality to find out whether the town planning scheme permits you to run your proposed business on the site is highly recommended prior to taking the matter any further.

If you are looking to build or renovate an existing building for the purposes of running your business, it will undoubtedly be in your best interest to use the services of an architect. By doing this, you will ensure that your proposed premises meet all of the required building codes right from the start.

The actual premises will, for example, need to comply with

- laws relating to health and safety,

- laws and/or town planning schemes relating to land-use rights,

- laws applicable to building control in compliance with national building regulations and the *Building Standards Act, 1977,*

- laws applicable to noise and air pollution, and

- laws applicable to public safety.

It will not only be very costly but will most probably set you back many months if, as a result of your not obtaining expert advice, you were to discover that the building did not meet all of the legal requirements. If you are in any doubt, contact your local authorities before you start building or renovating the premises. Find out the general requirements and then ensure that both your architect and builder are familiar with these regulations.

In the case of Jaque's Treats, Jaque will have to determine where she will process her preserved fruit, and what the legal implications of this will be. Is she allowed to process food where she is? Does she have a suitable building that meets the required food processing requirements? How will she make sure that she meets any health and safety requirements on her premises? Will she have to invest in any changes to existing buildings to make them legally complaints? If so, how much will this cost?

This chapter will guide you through some of the areas you will need to consider before building, renovating, or leasing your business premises.

6.3 Land and zoning requirements

If you are looking to purchase a property specifically for the purpose of opening a business, you will need to ensure that the zoning of the land permits the opening of such a business prior to concluding the purchase. It may, for example, be an infringement of local planning regulations or by-laws to start a business from a residence. Another example could be that a specific type of business may not be permitted on the premises you are considering.

- What do I need to do? Check the zoning and consent for use of the land before purchasing and or building.

- Who do I need to contact? The city or town council or municipality in your immediate area.

6.3.1 Restrictive conditions

If there is a restrictive condition in the title deed of the land you intend using (for example, the land may only be used for residential purposes), an application for the removal of the restriction or for rezoning can be made. The *Removal of Restrictions Act, 84 of 1967* empowers provinces to alter, suspend, or remove certain restrictions on land.

The zoning requirements, costs, and procedures will differ from region to region, and it will be necessary to contact the local municipality and/or provincial government for the exact details.

6.3.2 Application for removal of restrictive conditions

If the land is situated in an area governed by a local authority, the application for the removal of the restrictive condition or for rezoning should be lodged with this authority. Simultaneously, a copy of the application should be forwarded to the director-general of the province in which the land is located.

If the property is not situated in an area governed by a local authority, the application for rezoning will need to be lodged with the director-general of the province in which it is located. However, it is recommended that you start your enquiries with the local authority, as they will be in a position to advise you on how best to move forward.

On receipt of your application, the director-general requires that a notice is placed in both official languages in the *Provincial Government Gazette* of the province. The director-general also requires that a notice is placed twice (with an interval of one week between placements) in a newspaper widely circulated in the area in which the business is to be located. This notice will state that an application for the removal of a restriction on the land has been made, and that objections against the application may be lodged with the director-general on or before a specific date. This date will not be less than 21 days after the date of the last publication of the notice.

The director-general will also require that a copy of the notice be sent by registered post to every owner of land who is, or may be, directly affected by the application. This usually involves the immediate neighbours. In such an event, it would be wise to canvass the support and approval of the neighbours first. A written consent of the bondholder should accompany an application if a bond is registered over the business property. A copy of every objection received by the director-general will be sent to the applicant by registered post.

When dealing with the local authority, some municipalities expect the following special conditions to be met:

Submission of the following documentation together with the application for the alteration, suspension, or removal of the restriction on the land on which your business is to be located:

- the title deed to the property (this is registered with the Deeds Office when the application is submitted),

- proof of having placed the advertisements in the *Provincial Government Gazette* (as outlined above), and

- prints of the locality plan and a plan indicating the proposed rezoning. (A locality plan is available from the local municipality and indicates the position of the business stand in the town or city.)

In some instances, the applicant may be required to give reasons as to why the restriction on the land use should be altered, suspended, or removed.

It is important to take the following factors into account when applying for rezoning:

- The rate and tax base will usually change after rezoning, so this must be budgeted for in the business plan.

- If the premises of the business are leased, it might constitute a breach of the lease agreement to use them for business purposes or to make any additions or alterations to them. The lease agreement must provide for the establishment of a business and/or alterations should they be required.

- An application for special consent use, in terms of the *Planning and Development Act, 5 of 1998*, will have to comply with the requirements and procedures as outlined in the Act.

6.4 Business and directional signage

If the business is appropriately zoned, it is usually not necessary to get approval from your local municipality if you wish to erect signs on the actual property.

- What do I need to do? Apply for business and road directional signage
- Who do I need to contact? The city or town council or municipality in your immediate area.

For permission to erect directional signage on public roads leading to the business, the applicant will, in all probability, need to apply to the local authority responsible for roads management. As the method of application differs across the provinces and from region to region, it will be best for you to contact your local authority in order to ascertain the exact application process and procedure.

Note that, in terms of the national *Roads Act, 7 of 1998*, no signage (neither directional nor informative) may be located in such a manner that it becomes visible from a National Road unless it complies with certain requirements in terms of section 50 of the Act. The requirements cover the permissible location, size, and contents of the signs. Failure to comply will result in a letter from the National Roads Agency requiring the removal of the sign. Failing that, the Agency will remove the sign, costs will be recovered, and/or a fine will be imposed under the Act.

6.5 Access to and from a public road

If you are planning to build, you will probably require public access to your premises from a public road for use by your customers and suppliers and your own delivery vehicle(s). If you do not already have access to and from an existing public road, there are various limitations as to what is or is not permissible.

- What do I need to do? Obtain planning permission for access to and from a public road.
- Who do I need to see? Local/provincial and/or national roads authority.

Most of the limitations are concerned with public safety and will relate directly to the type or classification of road you intend accessing. It could be a local, provincial, or national road, and so the requirements will differ. The distances between the proposed entry point and potential danger points, such as blind corners, traffic lights, and pedestrian crossings, will also be taken into consideration.

Invariably, road access plans will form part of the building plans drawn up by the architect and will be approved or declined as the case may be by the local authority. It is important to note that local by-laws and even provincial requirements will differ, and it is therefore essential that you obtain authorisation from the appropriate authority prior to the building of the proposed access.

6.6 Freedom from a land claim

The government introduced land reform in 1994, and this is further derived from Section 25 of the *Constitution of South Africa, Act 108 of 1996.* When considering either purchasing land or an existing business, it is essential to ensure that there is no outstanding claim against the property.

> • What do I need to do? Establish freedom from a land claim.
>
> • Who do I need to contact? The Department of Land Affairs in Pretoria or the Land Claims Court in Randburg, Johannesburg

The Land Reform Programme consists of

* **land restitution**, which usually involves returning land lost because of racially discriminatory laws, although it can also be effected through compensation,
* **land redistribution**, which enables disadvantaged people to buy land with the help of a settlement or land acquisition grant, and
* **land tenure reform**, which aims to bring all people occupying land under one legal system of landholding. It will provide for diverse and secure forms of tenure, help resolve tenure disputes, and provide alternatives for people who are displaced in the process.

The Land Restitution Programme, which could impact on the sale or purchase of a particular property, originates from the Constitution and was established by the *Restitution of Land Rights Act of 1994*. The purpose of the programme is to assess the validity of claims, restore land, and/or pay financial compensation to people who were dispossessed of their land rights as a result of racially discriminatory laws and practices after 19 June 1913.

The Land Claims Court, situated in Randburg, is responsible for determining restitution and compensation for those who lost land as a result of forced removals. The court is required to be accessible to everyone and to establish processes that will enable it to make speedy decisions. Enquiries can be made through the court or directly with the Department of Land Affairs in Pretoria.

This would be particularly important to Jaque to ensure that her family farm is not subject to a land claim before she starts processing the fruit crop from the farm.

6.7 The environmental scoping report

Requirement	Authority	Location
Adherence to the various environmental conservation requirements	Local and/or provincial authorities	Various

The Minister of Environmental Affairs and Tourism has identified a number of activities that may have a detrimental impact on the environment and has therefore made provision for specific procedures that must be followed before any such activities are started. These provisions are contained in the *Environmental Conservation Act, 73 of 1989*, which is amended from time to time.

Bear in mind that, if you intend building on a piece of land that has not been built on before or if you intend making alterations to an existing building or grounds, these activities could result in a negative impact on the environment. Should this be likely, it will be very important to ensure that either you or your builder ascertains exactly what you are required to do in terms of the Act.

The more severe the impact on the environment, the more comprehensive the application procedures will be. The felling of one or two trees may only require a phone call and a visit from a representative of the local authority, whereas the building of a road will undoubtedly require the applicant to follow every condition of the Act. It is important to note that it is the authorities, and not the applicant, who will decide on whether or not an activity may or may not have an impact on the environment. There is no protection on the grounds of ignorance or error.

It is more than likely, should rezoning of land have taken place, that the applicant will be required to follow the complete procedure. It is recommended that pre-consultation with the authorities takes place prior to any application as, under certain circumstances, an exemption from the Act may apply.

Legal requirements will more often than not require the applicant to complete the following:

- a pre-consultation process with the local authorities to ascertain what level of application is likely to be required relative to the proposed undertaking,
- a plan of study for scoping report,
- a scoping report, and
- an environmental impact assessment (EIA) report.

The process is relatively complex, and it is therefore suggested that you approach an environmental specialist or legal consultant or that you receive confirmation from the appointed builder or architects that they are fully conversant with the requirements of the Act.

6.8 Registration in terms of the National Water Act

Requirement	Authority	Location
Registration requirements in terms of the national *Water Act*	Local Department of Water Affairs and Forestry	Various

South Africa's scarce water resources are under increasing pressure and will need to be wisely managed in the coming years. In order to achieve this, the Department of Water Affairs and Forestry needs to know how much water is being used, by whom, and where. The department can then ascertain how much water is actually available for use and effectively manage the future sustainability of the country's water resources.

The *Water Act, 36 of 1998* gives the Department of Water Affairs and Forestry the means to gather the required information for the optimal management of all of the country's water resources. The registration of water use is one of these tools.

All water users instructed to register have a statutory obligation to do so, and there are strict penalties prescribed within the Act for those who do not comply.

6.8.1 Registration

The following water users must register their water use: All water users, who do not receive their water from a service provider, local authority, water board, irrigation board, government water scheme or other bulk supplier and who are using water for

- irrigation,
- mining purposes,
- industrial use,
- feedlots, or
- in terms of a general authorisation.

Other uses which must be registered include

- diversion of rivers and streams,
- stream flow reduction activities,
- all tree planting for commercial purposes,
- discharges of waste or water containing waste,
- storage, which means any person or body storing water for any purpose (including irrigation, domestic supply, industrial use, mining, aquaculture, fishing, water sport, aesthetic value, gardening, landscaping, golfing, etc) from surface runoff, groundwater, or fountain flow in excess of 10 000 cubic metres
- local authorities and other bulk suppliers with their own water sources and purification works,
- controlled activities, such as irrigating with waste, power generation with water, atmospheric modification, or recharging an aquifer, and
- using water for recreational purposes.

Therefore, if you have a business that is likely to use water for recreation or consumption and you will be using your own water sources, you will have to register. This could include a fishing lodge with trout dams or other such facilities.

If you receive water from a local authority, a water board, an irrigation board, or another bulk water supplier, you do not need to register that use. The department will register you if required and send you a certificate or a semi-completed application to complete.

6.8.2 Contact details

You will be required to make contact with the regional office of the Department of Water Affairs and Forestry in the area in which your business is located. For contact information, access the national department's website at www-dwaf.pwv.gov.za.

6.8.3 The registration process

You will be required to complete and submit whichever form is appropriate to your circumstances. If you are in any doubt, it is recommended that you contact the appropriate regional office and discuss the matter with them. Once you have obtained confirmation on what you are required to do and/or which form or forms you are required to submit, you can download a copy or copies from the following website: www.dwaf.gov.za/Projects/WARMS.

Select the appropriate form or forms for completion and submit them to your Regional Water Affairs offices.

6.9 Submission of building plans

Requirement	Authority	Location
Submitting building plans for approval	The local authority in the area in which the building activity is to take place	Various

Building plans are required to conform with national, provincial, and local laws and by-laws. Therefore, it is important to ensure that the appointed architect or builder is totally familiar with these requirements and makes the necessary submissions, in terms of the proposed plans, to the appropriate local council or municipality.

Many aspects relevant to the building plans will be of concern to the local authorities. These could include the parking layout, turning and loading facilities, and street access. Bear in mind that parking facilities must be adequate and correspond with the size and nature of the business or establishment that you are planning.

In many cases, local by-laws differ from one council or municipality to another. Therefore, it is wise to ensure that the architect or builder is in possession of the specific local authority requirements and that they have been incorporated in the plans to be submitted. This will substantially reduce the potential for delays in obtaining approval. Examples of items covered by statutory requirements would include the provision of toilet facilities, fire escapes, and so on.

Formal approval will be required from the local authorities if extensions, changes to frontages, and structural alterations are to be made to an existing building. For example, if Jaque intends to make any changes to buildings on the farm, she will first have to get these alterations approved by the relevant authorities.

6.10 Fire regulations and requirements

Requirement	Authority	Location
Fire and safety regulations	Local authority – fire division	Various

6.10.1 Building regulations and safety provision

Occupational health and safety is not just to do with safe working practices but is equally applied to buildings and premises. For example, should an accident happen or a fire break out, legislation provides for the means of dealing with the emergency and for the safe evacuation of both employees and members of the public.

Once a building is complete or the business premises are ready for inspection, the owner or manager is required to contact the local fire department and request an inspection of the premises. If all is well they will, after inspection, issue a Fire Clearance Certificate.

6.10.2 Relevant codes of practice or SABS documents

Section 33 of the *Standards Act, 30 of 1982* makes provision for the South African Bureau of Standards (SABS) to apply for the inclusion of certain codes of practice into legislation. The codes of practice listed below have all been included in the law, and so adherence to these provisions is mandatory.

- SABS 543: Fire hose reels (with hose).
- SABS 1128: Fire-fighting equipment.
- SABS 1151: Portable fire extinguishers of the halogenated hydrocarbon type.
- SABS 1186: Symbolic safety signs.
- SABS 10105: The classification, use, and routine maintenance of portable fire extinguishers.
- SABS 0139: Fire detection and alarm systems.
- SABS 1475: Service and maintenance of portable fire-fighting equipment.
- SABS 0400: 'The Application of the National Building Regulations' from the *National Building Act, 103 of 1977*.

International hazard signs must be displayed where deemed necessary by the local authorities. The most important fire, evacuation, and first-aid requirements are briefly outlined below.

6.10.3 Fire and emergency services

The fire and emergency services work within the parameters of the *Building Regulation Act, 103 of 1977* together with 'The Application of the National Building Regulations'. The local fire authority will assist if you are in any doubt about the fire and emergency information requirements. There are, however, a few regulations that are easy to understand and apply.

For example, any form of gas installation on the premises must be inspected annually by the fire department. While carrying out this inspection, they will check the number of extinguishers available, check the maintenance and upkeep of the equipment, and assess any other potential fire hazards that may exist.

6.10.4 Provision of fixed fire-fighting equipment

Fire hydrants and hose reels must be provided in any building that exceeds 1 000 m² of floor area, or part thereof.

- Hose reels, for the purposes of fire fighting, must be installed in any building of two or more storeys in height or in any single-storey building of more than 250 m² at a rate of one hose reel for every 500 m² or part thereof of floor area of any storey.
- Any hose reel installed in such a building must comply with the requirements as laid down by the SABS.

6.10.5 Portable fire-fighting equipment

The SABS stipulates that any building must contain at least one 4.5 kg fire extinguisher per 200 m² of floor area. Many fire authorities will recommend dry powder extinguishers, as they are effective for all types of fires.

Fire extinguishers must be kept in approved, accessible positions, and must be routinely inspected and maintained by an approved service provider. Consult your local fire department for advice on positioning and number of extinguishers required. Fire blankets are not stipulated in the regulations, but they are highly recommended by the fire authorities, especially for use in kitchens.

6.10.6 Provision for means of escape

The SABS requirements also cover evacuation routes and fire escapes. When drawing up building plans for a workplace or a place of entertainment, ensure that your architect is conversant with the relevant safety codes and requirements.

Remember that all building plans will need to be approved by the local fire authorities.

A place of entertainment and a workplace must have at least two means of escape, which, with the approval of the fire authorities, may include the front door. Doors have to be within a certain width specification, depending on the number of people likely to occupy the premises.

The locking mechanisms on fire escape doors must be approved by the local fire authority. Some fire departments will not permit glass key boxes but will allow locking devices that are secured and operated from the inside.

Inspect your business premises to ensure that you are aware of where all the fire-fighting equipment, detection systems, and alarms are, and that they are all in good working order. Check that the fire extinguishers have been serviced.

6.10.7 Detection and alarm systems

Establishments are also required to have a manually activated audible alarm system that is approved by the SABS. There are no regulations providing for fire or smoke detectors in smaller establishments, but they are highly recommended by the fire authorities.

6.11 First-aid requirements

Requirement	Authority	Location
First-aid requirements	Local authority – fire and safety division	Various

The *Machinery and Occupational Safety Act, 6 of 1983*, General Safety Regulation R1031, makes the following stipulations with regard to the mandatory provision of first-aid supplies and equipment:

Taking into account the type of injuries that are likely to occur at a workplace, the nature of the activities performed and the number of employees employed at such workplace, the employer shall make sure that the first aid box or boxes contain suitable first aid equipment, which includes at least the equipment listed hereunder; and that such an employer shall make sure that only articles of equipment or medicines [are] kept in the first aid box or boxes.

Minimum contents of a first aid box

In the case of shops and offices, the quantities stated for items 1, 8, 9, 10, 14, 15, 17, and 18 may be reduced by half.

Item 1:   Wound cleaner/antiseptic (100 ml)

Item 2:   Swabs for cleaning wounds

Item 3:   Cotton wool for padding (100 g)

Item 4:   Sterile gauze (minimum quantity 10)

Item 5:   1 pair of forceps (for splinters)

Item 6:   1 pair of scissors (minimum size 100 mm)

Item 7:   1 set of safety pins

Item 8:   4 triangular bandages

Item 9:   4 roller bandages (75 mm x 5 m)

Item 10: 4 roller bandages (100 mm x 5 m)

Item 11: 1 roll of elastic adhesive (25 mm x 3 m)

Item 12: 1 non-allergenic adhesive strip (25 mm x 3 m)

Item 13: 1 packet of adhesive dressing strips (minimum quantity: 10 assorted)

Item 14: 4 first aid dressings (75 mm x 100 mm)

Item 15: 4 first aid dressings (150 mm x 200 mm)

Item 16: 2 straight splints

Item 17: 2 pairs large and 2 pairs medium disposable latex gloves

Item 18: 2 CPR mouth pieces or similar devices

6.12 Self-evaluation

1. You want to open a retail clothing store, and you are planning to rent premises. Complete a list of questions you intend asking the landlord before you sign a lease, to ensure that you will not fall foul of any law or regulation that governs

business premises.

2. What requirements would you recommend that Jaque investigates before establishing a food-processing enterprise on existing agricultural land?

3. Why is it important to ensure that your premises comply with health and/or fire regulations?

4. Under what circumstances do you think an enterprise would need an environmental scoping report?

7 Registration and licensing

7.1 Learning outcomes

After studying this chapter, you should be able to

- register the name of your business,

- register your business as a legal entity,

- apply for a trade or business licence,

- register your business for tax purposes,

- register for the Skills Development Levy, the Unemployment Insurance Fund, and the Workmen's Compensation Fund, and

- comply with the requirements of the *Employment Equity Act*.

7.2 Introduction

Most businesses, no matter how big or small, are required to register with certain government bodies and/or apply for certain licences in order to operate lawfully in South Africa. Unfortunately, there are a significant number of these registration and licensing requirements and they often depend on the type of industry and the nature and size of the business you plan to operate.

Some registration and licensing requirements are generic to all forms of business, others are industry specific, some are as a result of something you have decided to introduce into your business, and there are even one or two that may be product specific.

A typical generic registration requirement would be registering with the South African Revenue Services (SARS) for tax purposes. An industry-specific requirement would, for example, be registering with the Bargaining Council if you run a restaurant in Johannesburg. You may, for example, decide to play music in your retail shop for your customers and staff and in this case you would need to register with the South African Music Rights Organisation (SAMRO). A product-specific requirement would be registering a medicine (even traditional medicines) for commercial sale with the Medicines Control Council.

Each section in this chapter will deal with who should register and/or obtain a certain licence and how you should go about the registration process or application for that particular licence.

In the case of Jaque Khumalo, she will have to ask herself a number of questions in order to determine what registrations she will have to undertake. These questions include:

- What form of business have I chosen, and how do I reserve a name for Jaque's Treats?
- How do I register Jaque's Treats as a CC or company?
- What are my tax responsibilities?
- Where do I find these out and how do I register to pay tax?
- Must I pay VAT? If so, how? And how do I calculate it?
- What operating licences do I need to run my preserving operation lawfully?
- I am going to employ people to help me preserve my fruit – what do I have to do to protect them against future unemployment or accidents in the workplace?
- Do my employees have to pay income tax and how do I register them for that?

These and other similar questions will help her to figure out what she needs to do before she starts operating.

The following table provides an overview of registrations, showing the authorities concerned in each of the registration and licensing procedures.

Overview of registrations:

Companies and Intellectual Property Registration Office of South Africa (CIPRO)

- Register the name of a company or close corporation.
- Register a close corporation.
- Register a company.

Other licensing requirements

- Trade licence

South African Revenue Services (SARS)

- Register for company income tax.

- Register company as an employer.

- Register for value added tax.

- Register for the Skills Development Levy.

- Register for the Unemployment Insurance Fund (UIF).

The Workmen's Compensation Commissioner

- Register your business with the Workmen's Compensation Fund.

The Department of Labour

- Register in terms of the *Employment Equity Act*.

7.3 Registering the name of your business

In chapter 5 we covered the various options that an entrepreneur can choose from when establishing a small business. We looked at the differences between sole proprietorships, partnerships, close corporations, and companies. Having decided upon the structure most suited to your business, you are now going to have to decide on a name for your business and whether or not you are required to register that name.

Requirement	Authority	Contact details
Registering the name of your business	The Companies and Intellectual Property Registration Office of South Africa (CIPRO)	CIPRO Website: www.cipro.co.za Postal Address: PO Box 429, Pretoria, 0001 Physical Address: The DTI campus (Block F - Entfutfukweni), 77 Meintjies Street, Sunnyside, Pretoria Contact Centre: Tel: 0861 843 384 Fax: 0861 843 888

7.3.1 Who will I be dealing with?

When registering a name, you will be dealing with the Companies and Intellectual Property Registration Office (CIPRO) of South Africa, based in Pretoria. The reason why you register a name is to avoid duplication of names and to protect the name of your business to ensure that others do not use the same name at some time in the future.

The first point to note is that, if you have chosen to set up a proprietorship or a partnership, you will not be required to register the name of your business with CIPRO. However, if the structure you have decided upon is a close corporation or a company, you will be required to register the name.

7.3.2 What procedure must I follow to register?

For the purposes of registration, we will assume that you have chosen to form a close corporation or company for your business. To start with, CIPRO will require that you submit at least three alternative names when registering.

Don't forget that you will need to register the name of your proposed close corporation or company before registering the actual business. You can save yourself a lot of time when selecting the three required names by using the CIPRO website 'Name search' function at www.cipro.co.za. This will help you ascertain whether or not the names you have chosen have already been registered.

Once you have selected the required three names and have ensured that they are not already being used, you will need to obtain and complete form CK7, 'Application for Reservation of Name, or Translated Form, or Shortened Form'. This form can be obtained from the CIPRO office in Pretoria and can also be bought from stationers that supply legal forms, such as Waltons, Hortons, and some branches of CNA.

You can also fill in a similar document online, which is very easy to do, although you have to pay for the submission before CIPRO will process it.

Process for registration: online

1. First register with CIPRO as a customer, registering an 18-character code with them; the first six characters you make up yourself. This six-character code then becomes your customer code, so make sure that you use it in all correspondence with CIPRO. The next eight digits are the date of the registration (mm-dd-yyyy), followed by the payment number that day – usually

only one payment per day, so that would be 01. An example would be as follows: mouse2404200601.

2. Make payment of the fee to create your virtual bank account with them – this must be done before they will do any processing for you. You can make a physical deposit into their account, quoting your code, or you can make an electronic payment.

3. Fax proof of your payment (either your deposit slip or electronic payment proof) to CIPRO to activate your account, which should take 24–48 hours.

4. Only once your account is activated can you start submitting information online.

Process for registration: offline

If you are not going to submit online, the CK7 form must be completed in black ink, the writing must be legible and in capital letters, and a fee of R50.00 paid into the CIPRO bank account and proof of deposit submitted with your application.

You can submit the completed form through the post or drop it off at the CIPRO office in Pretoria.

Once the proposed name has been checked and approved, which will take around four to seven working days if not done online, the CIPRO office will forward you a confirmation letter indicating that the name has been reserved for you. If there is a query regarding the proposed names, the CK7 form will be returned to you for modification and re-submission.

Process:

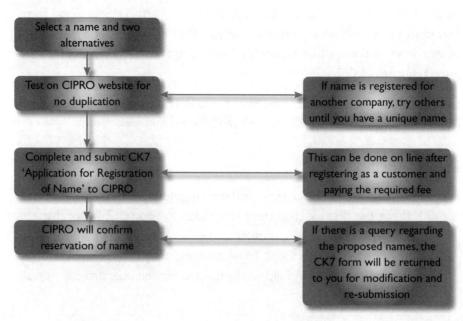

Select a name and two alternatives

Test on CIPRO website for no duplication → If name is registered for another company, try others until you have a unique name

Complete and submit CK7 'Application for Registration of Name' to CIPRO → This can be done on line after registering as a customer and paying the required fee

CIPRO will confirm reservation of name → If there is a query regarding the proposed names, the CK7 form will be returned to you for modification and re-submission

7.4 Registering your close corporation or company

Requirement	Authority	Contact details
Registering the business	The Companies and Intellectual Property Registration Office of South Africa (CIPRO)	CIPRO Website: www.cipro.co.za Postal Address: PO Box 429, Pretoria, 0001 Physical Address: The Dti campus (Block F - Entfutfukweni), 77 Meintjies Street, Sunnyside, Pretoria Contact Centre: Tel: 0861 843 384 Fax: 0861 843 888

7.4.1 Who will I be dealing with?

As with registering the name of your business, you will once again be dealing with the Companies and Intellectual Property Registration Office of South Africa (CIPRO), based in Pretoria.

Only a close corporation or a company is required to register. This is because both are treated as legal entities in South African law with their own legal personality. If you have formed a proprietorship or a partnership, you will not be required to register.

The registration process for a close corporation and a company are completely different and we have therefore covered each one separately.

7.4.2 How do I register a close corporation (CC)?

Only when the proposed CC's name has been approved and reserved can the actual registration process begin. Once the name has been registered, you will need to obtain and complete form CK1, 'Close Corporation Founding Statement'. Form CK1 can be obtained in exactly the same manner as you obtained form CK7 when registering the name.

Pages 1 and 2 of form CK1 must be completed by all close corporations. Page 3 is only applicable when there are more than four members in the CC. The CK1 must be completed in black ink and in block letters, and no amendments or alterations to the form will be accepted. The CK1 must be signed by all members, and three original copies must be submitted.

The original (no copies) completed CK1 form can be submitted either by post or in person to the Close Corporation Registration Office at the CIPRO building in

Pretoria. Currently, a payment of R100.00 is required and a number of payment options are available. Allow five to eight working days for processing. You must include a letter from the accounting officer confirming his or her appointment to the CC. On completion, a confirmation certificate that includes the registration number and registration date will be posted to the CC.

> If you personally take it to the CIPRO Offices in Pretoria, you will receive your certificate immediately.
>
> You can complete and submit a CK1 online. But the CK1 must then be printed, signed by the member(s), and submitted to CIPRO with the required letter from the accounting officer attached. (Note that this is not made quite clear on the website.)
>
> If at any time you have difficulty completing the forms or require any additional information, give CIPRO a call on 0861843384. They will not only assist you but provide you with a reference number that allows you to make follow-up calls without having to repeat yourself every time.

Process:

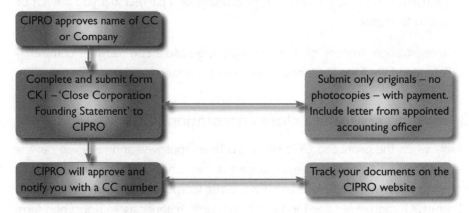

7.4.3 How do I register a company?

Registering a company can take many different forms, and it is a far more difficult and complex process than registering a close corporation. For this reason, we have chosen not to go into any lengthy detail. The registration procedure for a public or private company is extremely involved and will require the services of an attorney or chartered accountant.

Below is an example of the various requirements for registering the various types of company.

Documents	Purpose	Fees
CM5 (to be lodged in duplicate)	Application for reservation of a name	R50.00, original CM5 must be stamped
Power of attorney	Authorisation to act on registered and postal address	
CM22 (to be lodged in duplicate)	Notification of situation of registered and postal address	None
CM29	Return containing particulars of directors or accounting officer	None
CM46	Application for certificate to commence business	R60.00
CM47 (each director)	Statement by directors regarding adequacy or inadequacy of share capital	None
CM31 (to be lodged in duplicate)	Consent to act as auditor	None

Company category	Documents	Purpose	Fees
Company with share capital	CM1, CM2, 2A, 2B, 2C or 2D	Memorandum of association	R350.00 plus R5.00 per 1000 authorised capital in the case of par-value shares or R5.00 per 1000 in the case of no-par-value shares
Company without share capital	CM44B, 44C	Articles of association	None
Company limited by guarantee, or association incorporated by Section 21	CM3, 4, 4A, 4B	Certificate of incorporation and memorandum of association	None
Company adopting Table A or B	CM44	Articles of association	None
Company not adopting Table A or B	CM44A, 44C	Articles of association	None

Note: these details may be subject to change, so please check with CIPRO

7.5 Trade or business licences

Requirement	Authority	Contact details
Application for a trade licence	Local or district council/ municipality	Consult your local telephone directory or dial Telkom 1023 and enquire

Business or trade licence requirements are governed by the *National Business Act, 71 of 1991* and apply throughout the country. Permits and certificates, on the other hand, are issued in terms of local authority by-laws. These by-laws tend to differ from municipality to municipality. It is very important, when enquiring about or making application for your business or trade licence, that you establish whether or not your proposed business will require an additional permit or certificate of any kind, over and above the business or trade licence.

In terms of the *Business Act, 71 of 1991*, only businesses dealing in the following activities require a licence:

1. The selling or supplying of meals, take-aways or perishable foodstuff.

2. Operating:

   - Turkish baths, saunas and health baths,

   - massage or infra-red treatments,

   - male and female escorts,

   - three or more slot machines and electronic games,

   - three or more snooker or billiard tables,

   - nightclubs and discotheques, where live or loud music is played,

   - cinemas and theatres, and

   - adult premises.

7.5.1 Who will I be dealing with?

You will only be required to apply for a business or trade licence if you plan to open any one or more of the business types listed above. Depending on the location of your business or proposed business, you will either be dealing with a metropolitan council, a local municipality, or an area district council. Either way, and in 90 per cent of the cases, you will be dealing with the licensing office or licensing department in that particular municipality or council.

7.5.2 How do I apply for a licence?

The first step would be to contact your local council in order to ascertain whether or not you are required to apply for a trade licence. If the answer is yes, you will need to get hold of the appropriate application form or forms. On receipt of the form(s) you will need to complete them in full and provide any supporting documentation required. Some councils may charge you a fee for the forms, but this is not likely to cost you more than R30.00.

> When collecting the appropriate form, make sure that you establish exactly what, if any, additional documentation is required.

Once you have completed the form and attached the required documentation, return to the licensing office and submit the application. A once-off fee, which changes from year to year and possibly from council to council, must be paid. The fee is likely to range between R300 and R400.

7.5.3 Inspection and approval

On receipt of the completed form and supporting documentation, the licensing department will draft a report and send it to the various municipal departments involved in the process.

It will then be the responsibility of each of these departments to ensure that, as a result of a site inspection, your business complies with

- any law relating to health and safety,
- any law and/or town-planning scheme that relates to land-use rights,
- any law applicable to building control in compliance with the *National Building Regulations and Building Standards Act, 1977,*
- any law applicable to noise and air pollution, and
- any law applicable to public safety.

7.5.4 When do I receive the licence?

What normally happens is that each department sends out an inspector who, in turn, compiles a report confirming that your business conforms to the various regulations.

If, after the site inspection, the various department representatives indicate that additional requirements need to be met, the Trade Licence Department will send you notification. You will then need to comply with these additional requirements and arrange for a re-inspection.

Once the approval of the various departments has been received, the licensing department will issue you with a business or trade licence. The licence remains valid until such time as ownership changes or the activity specified on the licence changes. The licence is not transferable from one owner to another or from one set of premises to another. Once the trading licence has been granted, the premises may be inspected from time to time by a representative from any one or more of the departments.

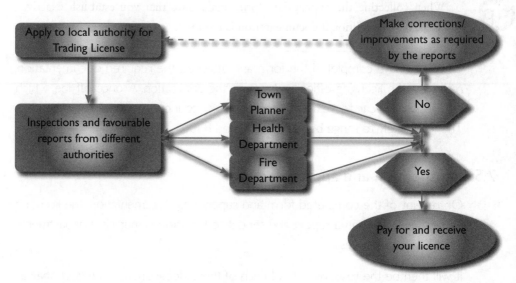

7.5.5 Permits and certificates

Here are a few examples of South African permit, licence, and certificate requirements:

- Permission to import chemicals
- Temporary/special permit to drive on a public road
- Local fishing vessel licence
- Certificate for acceptability of child care premises
- Permit to undertake commercial fishing
- Permit to operate a fish processing establishment
- Register a fishing vessel
- Commercial broadcasting service licence
- Permit to import a second-hand or used vehicle
- Community broadcasting service licence
- Export permit
- Mining permit/licence
- Register as a manufacturer/importer/builder of vehicles
- Motor trade permit and number
- Service stations licences

- Register as a manufacturer of number plates
- Registration for the carrying on and maintenance of a camping ground/caravan park business
- Register as a private higher education institution
- Registration for day care or child care
- Immigration permit (own business in partnership or cooperation)
- Register as a professional service provider
- Certificate of acceptability for food premises
- Mining/prospecting by small-scale miners
- Registration of homes for the aged
- Register a vehicle model
- Register premises to be used as dairy/milk shop
- Licence to operate an unreserved postal service
- Licence to operate a reserved postal service
- Certificate of acceptability as a milking shed

7.6 Registering for tax purposes

When it comes to income tax in South Africa, there are two processes that need to be followed. The first step is to register your company, close corporation, sole proprietorship, or partnership for income tax purposes. The second step, if you plan to engage employees, is to register your business as an employer. This will also cover the required registration for Unemployment Insurance and the Skills Development Levy.

7.6.1 Registering your business for income tax purposes

Income tax is the state's main source of income and is levied on taxable income in terms of the *Income Tax Act*. Income tax is levied on a variety of entities: individuals, companies, and trusts. This means that your small business – whether it takes the form of a private company, a sole proprietorship, a close corporation, or a partnership – will be required to register and pay income tax.

7.6.2 Who will I be dealing with?

You must register with your local Receiver of Revenue branch office as soon as you start your business. By the time you are required to register with the Receiver of Revenue, you will have decided on the most appropriate form of business for your new enterprise from the following: a company, a close corporation, a partnership, or a sole proprietorship.

Requirement	Authority	Contact details
Registration for income tax purposes	The nearest South African Revenue Services Office	Establish where your nearest SARS office is either via the telephone book or by going online to www.sars.gov.za – open 'contact us' and open 'List of Revenue Offices'

7.6.3 How do I register my company or close corporation with SARS for tax purposes?

Remember that, in this section, we are only looking at the registration of a new company or a new close corporation. For registering a sole proprietorship or partnership, please refer to the next section

The first step is to obtain and complete form IT/IB 77C or IT77C, as it is sometimes referred to. The form can be obtained online from the SARS website at www.sars.gov.za.

Complete the form in full, using capitals or block letters, and ensure that you provide all of the information requested.

As the IT/IB 77C or IT77C is fairly complex, it would be advisable to seek assistance from a qualified individual, such as an accountant, when completing the form. If this is not possible, it would be a good idea to visit your local SARS customer service counter where a qualified consultant will be able to assist you.

Once the form has been completed, together with the supporting documentation, you can post it or hand-deliver it to your local SARS branch office. Make sure that you provide all of the following required supporting documents:

- a copy of your CK document (this is the registration document you would have received from CIPRO when you registered your close corporation or company with them),
- a certified and legible copy of the IDs of all of the members of your close corporation or company, and
- any ONE of the following:
  - a cancelled cheque (probably the easiest),
  - a certified (signed and stamped by the bank manager) legible copy of a

bank statement clearly indicating the account holder's name, account number, and branch number, or

○ an official letter from your bank manager on a bank letterhead confirming your name, account number, and the bank's branch number.

Process:

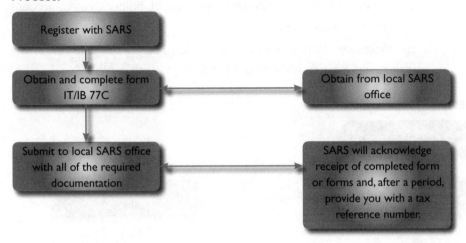

7.6.4 How do I register my sole proprietorship or partnership with SARS for tax purposes?

The first step in registering a sole proprietorship or a partnership is to obtain and complete form IT/IB77 in order to register as a provisional taxpayer. If you have a sole proprietorship, you will complete a single form. However, if you have a partnership, it is important to note that each partner must complete an IT/IB77 form.

The form can be obtained online from the SARS website at www.sars.gov.za. You can also obtain a copy from your local branch office of the Receiver of Revenue.

Complete the form in full, using capitals or block letters, and ensure that you provide all of the information requested. As the IT/IB 77 is fairly complex, it would be advisable to seek assistance from a qualified individual, such as an accountant, when completing the form. If this is not possible, it would be a good idea to visit your local SARS customer service counter where a qualified consultant will be able to assist you.

Once the form has been completed, together with the supporting documentation, you can post it to your local SARS branch office. Make sure that you sign the form and provide all of the following required back-up documentation:

• a certified and legible copy of your ID,

- income details for the last three years, either copies of IRP5s or IT3s, and
- if you have entered your bank details on the IT/IB77 form, you must provide any ONE of the following
  - a cancelled cheque (probably the easiest),
  - a certified (signed and stamped by the bank manager) legible copy of a bank statement clearly indicating the account holder's name, account number, and branch number, and
  - an official letter from your bank manager on a bank letterhead confirming your name, account number, and the bank's branch number.

Process:

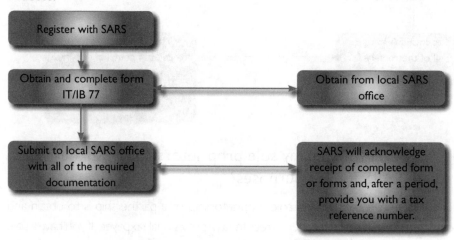

7.6.5 How do I register with SARS for employee tax, skills development, and UIF?

This section deals solely with registration as an employer for tax purposes. Therefore, we are going to assume that you will be engaging a number of employees in your business. No matter which form of business you have decided to adopt – whether it is a company, close corporation, sole proprietorship, or partnership – and if you intend to or have already engaged employees to work for you, you will need to register for employer tax purposes.

7.6.6 What do I need to do?

The first step in registering a company, close corporation, sole proprietorship, or partnership for employer tax purposes is to obtain and complete form EMP101e. The form can be obtained online at www.sars.gov.za. You can also obtain a copy from your local branch office of the Receiver of Revenue.

By completing and submitting the EMP101e form, you will not only be registering as an employer for tax purposes but you will automatically be registering in terms of the Skills Development Levy (SDL) and in terms of the requirements of the Unemployment Insurance Fund (UIF).

Complete the form in full, using capitals or block letters, and ensure that you provide all of the information requested.

> As the EMP101e form is fairly complex, it would be advisable to seek assistance from a qualified individual, such as an accountant, when completing the form. If this is not possible, it would be a good idea to visit your local SARS customer service counter, where a qualified consultant will be able to assist you.

Make sure that you sign the form and provide all of the required back-up documents. The list of attachments required is fairly lengthy and can be found on the last page of form EMP101e.

Once the form has been completed, you can post it to your local SARS branch office or alternatively hand the form and supporting documents in at your nearest Receiver of Revenue branch office. SARS will acknowledge receipt of your completed forms and, after a period, provide you with your tax reference number. Once your business has been registered in terms of form EMP101e, you will receive form EMP201 on a monthly basis from SARS. In this form, you will declare your tax liabilities for PAYE, SDL, and UIF.

Process:

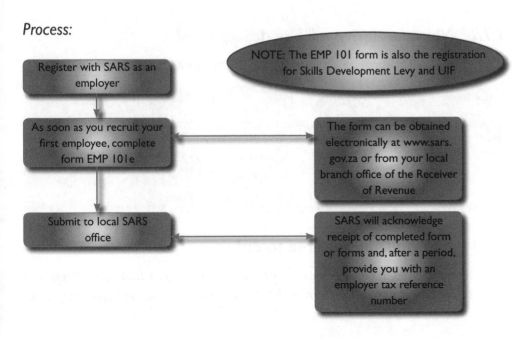

7.7 Registering your new business for the Skills Development Levy

In order to promote education and training in the workplace and to ensure the continual development and growth of the labour force in South Africa, the government has implemented an incentive scheme to employers in the form of the *Skills Development Act*.

Basically, the *Skills Development Act* requires that all employers pay 1% of their total employee payroll to the Receiver of Revenue on a monthly basis. This levy contribution is then paid over to what is called a Sector Education and Training Authority (SETA), whose responsibility it is to set standards, to monitor training, and to reward those businesses in a specific industry that carry out training and development in the prescribed manner. This is discussed in further detail in chapter 11.

Although the payment is a cost to your business you can, if you comply with the planning, training, and reporting requirements, reclaim up to 80% of the amount of levy that you have paid.

7.7.1 Who is required to register?

The law states that the levy must be paid by every employer who is registered with the Receiver of Revenue as an employer or has an annual payroll in excess of R500 000. If, however, you are not registered with SARS and your annual payroll is below R500 000, you will not be required to pay the levy.

7.7.2 Which authority will I be dealing with?

Once again, you will be dealing with the South African Revenue Services.

Requirement	Authority	Contact details
Registration under the Skills Development Act. Complete form EMP101e	The nearest South African Revenue Services Branch Office	Establish where your nearest SARS office is either via the telephone book or by going on line to www.sars.gov.za – open 'Contact us' and open 'List of Revenue Offices'

7.7.3 What will I be required to do?

Remember, as mentioned above, that when and if you have completed and submitted an EMP101e form to SARS, you will not only be registering as an employer for tax purposes but you will automatically be registering in terms of the Skills Development Levy (SDL).

Part 6 of form EMP101e deals with the levy, and, by completing the requirements correctly, SARS will automatically be able to ascertain whether or not you will be required to pay the levy.

7.8 Registering for Value-Added Tax

7.8.1 Who needs to register for VAT?

Any person who carries on an enterprise and whose total value of taxable supplies (taxable turnover) exceeds, or is likely to exceed, R300 000 in any 12-month period, must register for VAT. Registration will not be allowed if the annual turnover is below R20 000. In certain instances, the *VAT Act* allows a person to register voluntarily as a vendor even though his or her taxable turnover does not exceed or is expected to exceed R300 000 in a 12-month period.

It may be to your advantage for you to register voluntarily for VAT if you supply goods or services to another business that is VAT registered. This will allow them to claim the VAT incurred on the supply (i.e., input tax). If you supply services to non-vendors, (i.e., people who are not registered for VAT), it will generally not be to your advantage to register voluntarily for VAT.

It is important to note that, if your business income budget projects that your new company is not going to make over R300 000 or more in the first year of trading, and if you decide not to register on a voluntary basis, then you do not have to take the matter any further.

However, as the years go by and your company grows, you may exceed the R300 000 threshold and you will then be required to register.

It is important to note that the Receiver of Revenue often reviews the R300 000 annual figure and as a result it may go up or down. If you are unsure of the threshold, you should contact your local Receiver of Revenue branch office every year.

7.8.2 What is VAT all about?

Value added taxation (VAT) is a process whereby you are charged an additional 14%, on invoice, by your suppliers for services or products purchased by you in order to go about your business. You then charge your customer an additional 14% on the price of the services or products you supply to them. The difference between the tax you receive when your customers pay their accounts and the tax you have paid out when you have settled your supplier accounts is known as value added tax.

Essentially, the value added tax portion that you pay your suppliers over a given period is deducted from the value added taxation you charge your clients over the same period, and the balance is then paid over to the Receiver of Revenue.

You pay R100 for an item that you will use in production in your business. After processing, you sell this for R150. You paid 14% VAT on the original item. You receive 14% on the sales price of the item.

Purchase price of item: R100   VAT paid: R14.00   Price: R114.00

Sales price of item: R150   VAT charged: R21.00   Price: R171.00

How much VAT must you pay to the Receiver? The difference between the amount of VAT paid and the amount of VAT received is the answer. Every two months you have to add up all the VAT you have paid, and all the VAT you have charged, deduct the one from the other, and pay the difference to the Receiver.

7.8.3 Must I register for VAT?

This will depend on the particular circumstances of your business. You may be required to register by law, you may decide to register voluntarily, or you may not need to register at all.

There are two forms of VAT registration:

- **Compulsory.** This applies to any person who runs a business whose total value of taxable supplies or taxable turnover exceeds, or is likely to exceed, R300 000 in any 12-month period. Don't forget that, although you may not qualify for compulsory registration at present, as the years go by and your business grows, you may exceed the R300 000 threshold and you will then be required to register.

- **Voluntary.** Under certain circumstances, the *VAT Act* allows a person to register his or her business even although the taxable turnover does not exceed or is not expected to exceed R300 000 in any 12-month period.

There are a number of conditions under which you can voluntarily register for VAT, the most likely one being applicable to any person who carries on an enterprise in which the total value of taxable supplies (taxable turnover) exceeds R20 000 (but does not exceed R300 000) in the preceding 12-month period. A quick call to your local SARS office will clarify the situation for you. However, it is important to note that no registration will be allowed if your annual turnover is below R20 000.

7.8.4 Who do I contact?

Requirement	Authority	Contact details
Registration as a VAT vendor.	The nearest South African Revenue Services Branch Office.	Establish where your nearest SARS office is either via the telephone book or by going online to www.sars.gov.za – open 'Contact us' and open 'List of Revenue Offices'.

How to find your local SARS office: For contact information addresses and phone numbers, either consult your local telephone directory or go online to www.sars.gov.za – click on 'Contact us' at the top of the home page, go to 'Contact a SARS Office', and then click on 'List of Revenue Offices'.

7.8.5 What will I be required to do?

Having ascertained whether or not you are required to register, or if you have decided to register voluntarily, you will need to obtain and complete the necessary form.

Requirement	Authority	Contact details
Registration as a value added tax vendor.	If your business exceeds or is likely to exceed the R300 000 threshold, obtain and complete form VAT 101. The form can be obtained online at www.sars.gov.za or from your local branch office of the Receiver of Revenue.	Complete the form in full, ensuring you provide all of the information requested honestly and correctly. Once completed, hand the form in at your nearest Receiver of Revenue branch office. They in turn will acknowledge receipt of your completed form or forms and, after a period, provide you with a VAT tax reference number.

The registration form VAT 101 can be obtained online at www.sars.gov.za or from your local SARS branch office. It may well be a good idea, when collecting the VAT 101 form from SARS, to ask to speak to a client services consultant who will guide you through completion of this fairly complex form.

7.8.6 SARS VAT package for small business

SARS also offers certain small businesses a 'small retailers' VAT package'.

This package is a simpler VAT management system for small retailers, and forms part of SARS' drive to assist small businesses. If you qualify for the package, it will allow you to manage the day-to-day VAT requirements without detailed record keeping or having to buy expensive cash registers to keep track of sales on the various types of product you sell.

The package includes a free set of pre-printed books in which you keep track of the stock you buy and of your daily sales. In short, you get to spend more time and money growing your business. Remember that you will need to register for VAT first before you can apply for the package. However, when you visit the SARS branch office near you, ask for more information about the package.

Process:

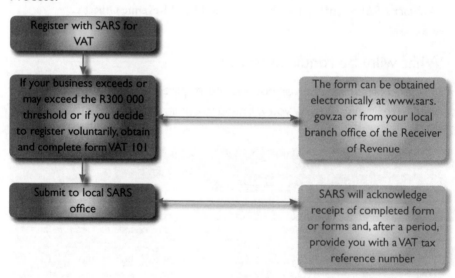

7.9 Registering your business and employees with the Unemployment Insurance Fund

The Unemployment Insurance Fund insures employees against the loss of earnings due to termination of employment, illness, and maternity leave. A monthly contribution has to be made by the employer (1%) and the employee (1%), based on the earnings of the employee. The contributions are calculated as a percentage of the remuneration paid to the employee for services rendered.

The main purpose of unemployment insurance is to ensure that employees who are contributors have access to the Unemployment Insurance Fund and to financial aid under certain circumstances.

7.9.1 Who is required to register?

The *Unemployment Insurance Act* and the *Unemployment Insurance Contributions Act* apply to all employers and workers, with the exception of

- workers working less than 24 hours a month for an employer,
- learners,
- public servants,
- foreigners working on contract,
- workers who get a monthly state (old age) pension, or
- workers who only earn commission.

As soon as you engage one or more employees who qualify, and provide them with remuneration in either cash or kind, you are required by law to register both your business and employees for Unemployment Insurance.

It is the responsibility of the employer to register both the business and the employees and to ensure that the information provided to the fund is updated every month should any changes have taken place. For example, if an employee leaves your employ or if you recruit new employees, you are required to make the necessary changes on the applicable form each month as and when they occur.

7.9.2 Which authority will I be dealing with?

Remember that, if you have registered as an employer, you will automatically have registered for UIF by completing form EMP 101e and, of course, will once again be dealing with the South African Revenue Services (SARS).

Requirement	Authority	Contact details
Registration under the Unemployment Insurance Act	The nearest South African Revenue Services Branch Office or the Unemployment Insurance Commissioners Office	Establish where your nearest SARS office is either from the telephone book or by going online to www.sars.gov.za – open 'Contact us' and open 'List of Revenue Offices'

7.9.3 What will I be required to do?

As an employer, you will automatically have registered for UIF when you completed form EMP101e. If you are not registered with SARS for employees' tax and/or Skills Development Levy purposes (by means of an EMP 101e registration form), you must register directly with the UIF Commissioner by completing and submitting form UI-8.

Unlike the registration of your business, registering your employees is an ongoing process and is updated every month. To register your employee or employees, you will need to complete Form UI 19, 'Information of Employee'.

Both forms are available online at www.labour.gov.za or can be obtained from your nearest labour centre.

7.10 Registering your business with the Workmen's Compensation Fund

The objective of the fund is to provide compensation for any disablement caused by injuries and/or diseases that are sustained in the workplace. These injuries or illnesses often come about as a result of the type of work or working conditions under which the employee is placed.

All employers must register with the Compensation Fund so that their workers can claim compensation for occupational injuries and diseases sustained at work. As an employer, and for as long as you are registered, you will be protected against a possible civil claim if an employee is injured while working for you.

7.10.1 Who is required to register?

All employers who employ one or more workers in connection with their business are required to register with the Compensation Fund. All registered employers (with a few exceptions) pay an annual assessment fee. A separate registration is necessary for each separate branch of a business, unless an arrangement with the Compensation Commissioner has been made for combined registration.

7.10.2 Which authority will I be dealing with?

Requirement	Authority	Contact details
Registration for Workmen's Compensation	The Compensation Commissioner's Office and or any labour office	Establish where your nearest labour office is from the telephone book or by going online to www.labour.gov.za and opening 'Centres & offices'

You will be dealing with the Compensation Commissioner, who is based in the offices of the national Department of Labour in Pretoria. However, in order to register, you may contact the labour centres or provincial labour offices nearest to you. Provincial and local labour offices are located throughout the country. To obtain the physical address and/or contact details of an office near you, you can either refer to your local telephone directory or go online to www.labour.gov.za.

7.10.3 What will I be required to do?

You will need to obtain and complete form WAS2 'Registration of Employer with Compensation Fund' from either the Commissioner's Office in Pretoria or one of the labour centre offices near you.

Alternatively, you can obtain it online at www.labour.gov.za. Click on 'Compensation for Occupational Injuries and Diseases' on the left of the home page.

Once you have obtained a copy of the form, make sure that you

- fill in all of the questions on the form (if the Compensation Fund has to follow up on information that you did not fill in, it will take a lot longer to be register),
- complete the form in capital letters,
- attach a copy of the registration certificate from the Registrar of Companies if you have set up a company or close corporation, and
- attach a copy of your ID document if you have set up a sole proprietorship or copies of the IDs of all of the partners if you have set up a partnership.

Once you have completed the form in full and in capitals and have attached the required documents, you can post it either to the Compensation Commissioner in Pretoria or to your local labour centre. Alternatively, you can drop it off at either of them.

The Compensation Commissioner's offices will process the form and advise you when your business has been registered. You will not be required to make any payment at this time. Wait for the notice of assessment.

Process:

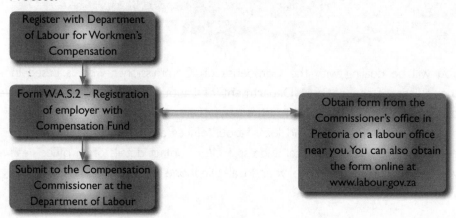

7.11 Compliance with the Employment Equity Act

7.11.1 Who is required to register?

The *Employment Equity Act* applies to all employers, workers, and job applicants, but not members of the

- South African National Defence Force,
- South African National Intelligence Agency, and
- South African Secret Service.

The Employment Equity Act applies to

- employers with 50 or more workers, or whose annual income is more than the amount specified in Schedule 4 of the Act (see details from the Schedule below),
- municipalities,
- organs of state,
- employers ordered to comply by a bargaining council agreement, and
- any employers who volunteer to comply.

The following details are from Schedule 4 of the *Employment Equity Act* : 'Turnover threshold applicable to designated employers':

Sector or sub-sectors in accordance with the standard industrial classification	Total annual turnover
Agriculture	R2 m
Mining and Quarrying	R7.50 m
Manufacturing	R10 m
Electricity, Gas and Water	R10 m
Construction	R5 m
Retail and Motor Trade and Repair Services	R15 m
Wholesale Trade, Commercial Agents and Allied Services	R25 m
Catering, Accommodation and other Trade	R5 m
Transport, Storage and Communications	R10 m
Finance and Business Services	R10 m
Community, Special and Personal Services	R5 m

7.11.2 Which authority will I be dealing with?

Requirement	Authority	Contact details
Compliance with the Employment Equity Act	The nearest Labour Centre to your business	Establish where your nearest Labour Centre is either via the telephone book or by dialling Telkom enquiries on 1023

You will be dealing with the Department of Labour in Pretoria or any one of the labour offices near you. Complete form EEA2 – Employment Equity Report.

7.11.3 Why am I required to register?

The purpose of the *Employment Equity Act* is to eliminate employment discrimination and to ensure equity in the workplace. The objective of the Act is to be achieved through the promotion of equal opportunity, fair treatment, and the elimination of unfair employment practices.

7.11.4 What will I be required to do?

If you have fewer than 50 employees and your total annual payroll is less than the turnover threshold applicable to your specific industry (see the table of details above), the *Employment Equity Act* will not apply to your business. However, irrespective of the number of workers you employ, you can voluntarily comply with the requirements of the Act.

Employers who are required to comply and those who choose to voluntarily comply are required to forward an employment equity report to the Department of Labour.

- Employers with less than 150 workers must send their reports within 12 months after they become employers, and thereafter every two years on the first working day in October.

- Employers with more than 150 workers must send their reports within six months after they become employers, and thereafter every year on the first working day in October.

The *Employment Equity Act* requires designated employers to send employment equity reports to the department. If you are required to comply, or if you choose to comply, you will need to obtain a copy of either form EEA2 (both big & small business) or form EEA2A (for small businesses). These forms give the format for employment equity reports, incorporate the reporting requirements, and contain the progress report that has to be completed.

These forms can be obtained online at www.labour.gov.za – click on 'Employment Equity' and click on Form EEA2 or EEA2A, 'Employment Equity Report'. You can also obtain copies of form EEA2 or EEA2A from your nearest labour office.

Once the form has been completed, you are required to post it to Employment Equity Registry, Department of Labour, Private Bag X117, Pretoria 0001, or you can e-mail it to ee@labour.gov.za

Process:

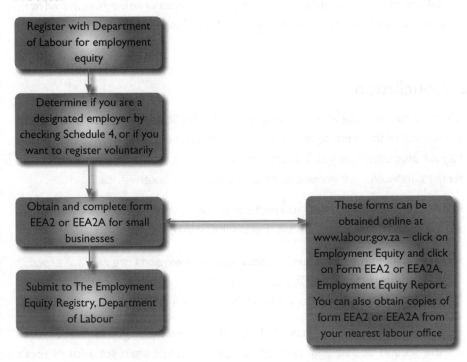

Register with Department of Labour for employment equity

↓

Determine if you are a designated employer by checking Schedule 4, or if you want to register voluntarily

↓

Obtain and complete form EEA2 or EEA2A for small businesses ⟷ These forms can be obtained online at www.labour.gov.za – click on Employment Equity and click on Form EEA2 or EEA2A, Employment Equity Report. You can also obtain copies of form EEA2 or EEA2A from your nearest labour office

↓

Submit to The Employment Equity Registry, Department of Labour

Do

1. **What will it take to make your business legal?**

   Fill in the following table to show what legal requirements there will be for your business, how much it will cost to meet each requirement, and how long each will take to put in place.

Legal requirements for this type of business	Cost	How long it takes to get the necessary permit/licence/qualification/insurance

2. How much will it cost me all together to make my business legal?

3. How long will it take to make my business legal?

Ask people who are already in this type of business or ask a business advice centre about legal requirements, costs, and how long it takes.

7.12 Conclusion

It is important to note, as mentioned in the introduction, that it is nearly impossible to cover all of the licensing and registration requirements that might be applicable to your proposed business. This chapter has covered those requirements that are likely to apply and are generic to most businesses in South Africa.

For further information, and to ensure that you have covered every angle, here are a few additional organisations that will be able to assist you

- **The Small Enterprise Development Agency, www.seda.org.za** Have a look at the various sections, but 'Topics' in particular, as it gives you a lot of information on various industry sectors, who to contact, and information on starting up.

- **The Department of Trade & Industries, www.thedti.gov.za** If you go to the section dealing with Business Support, you will again get a lot of useful information on whom to contact and who can assist you.

The following organisations will assist you in various ways or will provide or assist you to find the information you are after.

- **Chambers of Commerce and Industry South Africa (CHAMSA) www. chamsa.org.za** This is the independent umbrella body of the four national chambers, FABCOS, AHI, NAFCOC, and SACOB (they are listed individually below).

- **Foundation of African Business and Consumer Services (FABCOS) www. mbendi.co.za** This is an umbrella body of black business organisations which is active in the informal sector of the South African economy.

- **Afrikaanse Handelsinstituut (AHI) www.ahi.co.za** The AHI is a multi-sectoral employer organisation, involved in all sectors of the economy except primary agriculture.

- **South African Chamber of Business (SACOB) www.sacob.co.za** SACOB represents almost 100 local business chambers around South Africa.

- **National African Federated Chamber of Commerce and Industry (NAFCOC) www.nafcoc.org.za** NAFCOC represents the interests of small, micro, and medium-sized enterprises and black economic empowerment companies.

- **Black Management Forum (BMF) www.bmfonline.co.za** The BMF helps to empower managerial leadership (mainly among black people in corporations), as well as to develop ownership and creation of managerial structures and processes that reflect the demographics and values of the wider society.

7.13 Self-evaluation

1. Once you have read through this chapter, draw up a checklist of all the registrations that you will most likely have to undergo in order to make your business legally compliant. The following template may help you:

Registration requirement	Agency & local contact details	Form or document	Completed	Date
1.				
2.				
3.				

2. What registrations are you likely to have to submit to the Receiver of Revenue?

3. What does CIPRO stand for, and what are its functions?

4. What registrations do you have to submit to the Department of Labour and its agencies?

Section 3:

Business start-up

8 Operational contracts

8.1 Learning outcomes

After you have studied this chapter you should be able to

- enter into the following contracts with an understanding of what they entail:

  o sales contracts,

  o credit agreements,

  o leases,

  o insurance contracts,

  o employment contracts,

  o franchise contracts, and

- estimate whether you have adequate insurance for yourself and your business.

8.2 Introduction

When you start up or are running your own small business, you will often have to enter into a few basic legal contracts in order to protect or grow your enterprise. These basic contracts or legal agreements include, but are not limited to,

- **contracts:** lease, sales, and franchise, etc.,
- **insurance:** stock, public liability, vehicle, and
- **purchasing:** contract of purchase.

Jaque may have to enter into a rental agreement for the farm buildings where she will make her fruit preserves, she will have to buy supplies – sugar, jars and bottles, labels, boxes for shipping, and so on. She may have to buy a vehicle for deliveries, and insure that vehicle, insure her equipment, premises, and stock, and much more. Jaque will need to have a basic but thorough understanding of the ins and outs of each of these legal agreements so that she protects herself and her business.

Each contract gives certain rights and responsibilities to the contracting parties, and it is important for anyone signing a contract to know what these are, and what the contract expects of them.

This chapter will take a brief look at the various types of contract and provide you with information covering the contents and various legal obligations. It is important to note that, although this chapter will give you a good idea about what you should keep in mind when entering into an agreement, it does not serve as a comprehensive guide. For further advice, you should consult a professional legal consultant or lawyer.

8.3 Contracts

All businesses have to buy products and services from other businesses. When setting up a business, you will probably need to buy office equipment or furniture, and will also need operating equipment or production materials. All of these items will be supplied by other companies, and in many cases you may have to enter into some form of agreement or even sign a contract.

Restaurateurs, for example, will often be required to enter into supply contracts with butchers, grocers, and other providers of food and beverage products. When starting up a restaurant, many owners will also enter into contracts or lease agreements for buying or hiring equipment for their kitchens, restaurants, or bar areas.

A small factory may enter into a service agreement with a company to provide a cleaning service for its offices and production areas. Many business owners will want to protect their properties and products and as a result find themselves negotiating an agreement with a security company to supply this service.

You may be looking to outsource a number of your business requirements to specialists such as lawyers and accountants, who will then assist you in running your business. Some entrepreneurs may need the services of an architect or advertising agent, or may plan to rent their premises from a landlord. All of these aspects will involve commercial contracts, in one form or another, between you and other organisations.

D

All agreements or commercial contracts must comply with generally accepted requirements for them to become what is termed a **valid contract**.

However certain specific principles have evolved over the years concerning the most commonly concluded contracts. These contracts are known as specific or named contracts. For a contract to qualify as a **specific** or **named** contract, certain additional characteristics or requirements (essentialia) must be present.

The reason for classifying a contract as a specific or named contract is that certain naturalia or natural consequences could flow from that contract. These consequences regulate the relationship between the parties and cover certain aspects that the parties may not have regulated between themselves.

For example, if the parties to a contract of sale have not agreed when payment will be made, it is automatically assumed that payment will take place at the same time as the delivery of the product or service purchased. Therefore, it would be deemed to be a cash sale and not a credit sale. It is also evident from this example that the parties may have made other arrangements. For example, they may have agreed that payment will take place only at the end of the month.

8.4 Contract of sale

Certain types of contract are concluded more often than others. Typical examples of these would be contracts of sale, of lease, and of employment. Of these, the contract of sale is probably the most common. It is almost impossible to carry on any kind of business without either buying or selling products and services from time to time.

D

A **contract of sale** may be defined as a contract in which one party (the seller) undertakes to deliver the merx to another party (the buyer or purchaser), and the purchaser, in exchange for this, agrees to pay the seller a certain sum of money (the purchase price).

The term **merx** refers to the item that is purchased, and may consist of movable or immovable goods, or may even be an incorporeal thing such as a claim or a patent.

> **Incorporeal** describes something that is not material or physical; another word for this is intangible.

Not only must a contract of sale comply with the general requirements as mentioned above but, in addition, the parties must agree on two further essential characteristics, being the merx and the purchase price. This must occur before the contract can be described as or treated as a valid contract of sale. Consensus regarding the purchase price and the product or service sold shows that a contract of sale has been concluded and distinguishes it from other types of contract. They are, therefore, the *essentialia* of a contract of sale.

> **Essentialia** are certain additional characteristics or requirements of a specific type of contract, such as the length of a lease in a lease agreement, the price of the merx in an agreement of sale, and so on.

Jaque will be buying and selling: buying sugar, jars, labels, and so on, and selling her finished product, which is her preserved fruit. She will therefore enter into formal or informal contracts of sale.

8.4.1 The merx

A valid contract of sale can only exist if there is agreement with regard to the merx. The merx, therefore, must be definite or ascertainable (able to be verified).

The merx is 'definite' if it is mentioned by name in an agreement; for example, 'a red 2004 Toyota Corolla 1600 Sport'. It is also definite if the parties are in agreement about the product or service being sold.

The merx is 'ascertainable' (able to be verified) if it is described by number, weight, or measure together with a specific description of the product or service. Examples are '10 only Kingpin double beds' or 'fifty litres of Everfresh low-fat milk'. For Jaque, it may be to buy 24 X 250 ml glass jars, or selling 24 X 250 ml jars of mango chutney.

Nearly anything may be sold, provided that it can form part of one's patrimony, which means that it can be owned by someone. The merx may consist of movable or immovable goods or may even be an incorporeal or intangible object or article such as a claim or a patent.

Patrimony refers to an estate, a right, or an inheritance

All contracts must be lawful. No contract will be upheld where the law prohibits the sale of the merx, as in the case of illegal drugs, for example.

8.4.2 The purchase price

An essential requirement for a contract of sale is that a price for the merx has been agreed upon. Like the merx, the purchase price must be definite or ascertainable. Therefore, the parties have to agree on an amount, stipulate a price per unit, or confirm a method by which the purchase price will be determined. For Jaque, this may be the 250 ml jars of mango chutney selling at R10.95 each.

It often happens that commercial goods that are in limitless supply are bought and sold without any explicit reference being made to their price. A typical example would be when a person enters a shop and buys an article that does not have a price tag. A valid contract nonetheless comes into being, and the parties are deemed to have agreed on the price for the merx.

There are many different forms of price, as illustrated in the table below.

Forms of price	
Term	**What is given in return**
Price	Product or service
Tuition fee	Education
Rent	Place to live
Interest	Use of money
Fee	Professional services
Fare	Transport
Toll	Use of roads
Rate	Hotel rooms
Dues	Membership
Commission	Salesperson's services
Salary	Work (monthly)
Wage	Work (weekly)
Bribe	Illegal action

(Adapted from Van der Walt et al., 1995, p. 420)

8.4.3 The rights and duties of the purchaser and the seller

A contract of sale has important practical legal consequences. The delivery of the merx and the payment of the purchase price are part of any contract of sale.

It often happens that the parties to a contract of sale only agree on the two essential characteristics of a contract of sale. They might not consider a number of additional matters that are potentially relevant; for example, whether or not the merx has to be paid for in cash, in what way delivery is to take place, or what would happen if the merx were destroyed before it could be delivered to the purchaser.

South African common law provides a legal framework for contracts of sale, and if the parties do not make arrangements to the contrary, these natural consequences (naturalia) will always apply.

Naturalia is a term for the natural consequences of a contract. An example is the consequence that, after a contract of sale, the merx is owned by the buyer.

8.4.4 The common-law rights of the purchaser

Common law deems that the purchaser is entitled to

- delivery of the merx,
- preservation of the merx pending delivery,
- a merx free from latent defects, and
- be protected by the seller against eviction.

'As is', or 'voetstoots' sales: These are sales in which a guarantee against latent defects may be excluded from a contract of sale. The usual way is to state that the article is sold 'voetstoots' or 'as is'. The purchaser then has no legal remedies if the merx has a latent defect, except where the seller knew of the defect – in which case the purchaser will be entitled to claim damages.

8.4.5 The common-law rights of the seller

The seller is entitled to payment of the purchase price by the purchaser. This is the most important obligation of the purchaser and cannot be excluded from the contract by the parties. The payment of an agreed sum of money is one of the essential characteristics of a contract of sale.

8.4.6 The transfer of ownership

When a contract of sale is executed in full and without complications, the purchaser acquires ownership of the merx. The transfer of ownership is usually the primary objective of the parties to a contract of sale.

The transfer of ownership is regulated by the rules of the law of property. One of the ways in which a person can obtain ownership of a movable corporeal item is by its transfer to him or her by another person.

- Immovables, such as land and buildings, are transferred by way of registration in a Deeds Office.
- Ownership will transfer when the purchase price is paid or security given for the payment thereof or when credit has been granted. If it is a cash sale, ownership will pass only once the purchase price is paid. In the case of a credit sale – that is, where the seller has given time extension for the payment of the price – ownership will transfer on delivery.

> **Registration:** Immovables, such as land, are transferred by being registered in the name of the purchaser. As soon as the transfer is registered in a Deeds Office, transfer of ownership takes place.

8.4.7 Delivery

Movable property has to be delivered to the transferee. There are various forms of delivery that you may encounter in small business transactions.

- **Actual delivery:** This is the most common form of delivery, and entails the physical handing over of the merx by the seller or the seller's representative to the purchaser. This is normal in wholesale or retail trading activities.
- **Symbolic delivery:** Here the merx is not physically handed over to the purchaser, but something else is delivered to the purchaser that enables him or her to obtain control of the merx; for example, the seller of a shop hands over the keys of the premises to the purchaser.
- **Delivery with the long hand:** This entails the pointing out of the merx and that it is being made available to the purchaser. This method is used where the merx is too large or heavy to be handed over physically, such as cattle in a kraal, for example.
- **Delivery with the short hand:** This form of delivery occurs where the purchaser is already in possession of the merx, but he or she is not as yet

the lawful owner. Only at a later stage does the purchaser become the lawful owner. For example, Lulama borrows a car from Billy, and while she has it, they agree that she may buy it from him. She therefore does not take delivery of the vehicle as she already has it in her possession.

For a sale to be valid, the following legal requirements are most important:

- **The seller must be the owner:** If the seller is not the owner of the merx, he or she cannot transfer ownership to the purchaser. The legitimate owner can claim back the item from the purchaser even if the purchaser obtained the item in good faith and has paid for it. An example is when Amina buys a car from Jan in good faith, but the car was in fact stolen from Sipho. Sipho can therefore claim the car back from Amina.

- **Payment of the purchase price:** For the transfer of ownership, it is required that the purchase price be paid or that the seller has given the purchaser credit or has agreed security for the payment of the item. If there is nothing to indicate anything else, it is accepted that a contract of sale is concluded on a cash basis. In the case of a credit sale, ownership will pass on at the time the merx is delivered.

1. Explain the concept of merx.

2. What types of goods or products would you buy with a voetstoets clause?

3. How does ownership of land or buildings pass from the seller to the buyer?

8.5 Credit agreements

A credit agreement is not a specific or named contract, as is the case with a contract of sale or a lease agreement. A credit agreement is any contract in terms of which the parties agree that payment will take place at a future date. The seller thus extends credit to the purchaser for the contract price. A credit agreement is the opposite of a cash agreement.

A credit agreement enables the purchaser to obtain the goods or services immediately, while delaying payment or settling the cost over an agreed period of time. In your business, you are very likely to make use of credit options from suppliers as well as extending credit to your own clients.

Jaque may sell her Treats to her clients on account – therefore on a credit basis – and they will settle with her on a monthly basis. She may also buy goods on credit from the local co-op, and settle her account with them at the end of the month.

As a small business owner, you are likely to encounter credit agreements on a regular basis. Therefore, the more you know about them the better. Legislation has been passed to protect the consumer against any unlawful or unfair business practice. You, as the purchaser, are therefore protected if you are buying anything on credit and, likewise, your customers are protected when buying items from you.

You may agree to buy goods from your suppliers on credit and pay them at the end of the month. You may also agree to sell goods on credit and permit your customers to pay you at the end of the month. You may even permit your customers to settle their accounts over a six-month period.

Consumer protection

Legislation has been introduced to protect the consumer in certain credit agreements. This legislation can protect the consumer by prescribing formalities for contracts, prohibiting certain terms, and regulating certain consequences of the contractual relationship. Measures have also be introduced in an attempt to prevent overspending by consumers, for example by prescribing a relatively high deposit and restricting the period within which the price should be paid.

In South Africa, the most important consumer protection laws in terms of credit agreements are

- the *Credit Agreements Act, 75 of 1980*, which regulates certain transactions for the sale and lease of movable property and for the supply of services,

- the *Usury Act, 73 of 1968*, which regulates the finance charges in respect of certain credit, leasing, and money-lending transactions, and

- Chapter 2 of the *Alienation of Land Act, 68 of 1981*, which protects the purchaser of immovable property intended for residential use.

The legislation applies mostly to durable or long-lasting consumer items such as motor vehicles, furniture, and electrical equipment, and only to contracts extending over a period of longer than six months and where the cash price is R500 000 or less. These Acts generally do not apply where the state or a government body is the creditor.

It is important to note that the government is currently revisiting all of the existing consumer protection legislation with a view to combing the requirements into a single statute.

8.5.1 The form and content of credit agreements

Formalities

There are certain requirements for credit agreements. Credit agreements must

- be in writing,
- be in the official language requested by the credit receiver,
- be signed by or on behalf of all of the parties involved,
- state the names and addresses of the parties,
- clearly describe the goods or services to which the agreement relates, and
- state the amount of the deposit.

> The **parties to a credit agreement** are the credit grantor and the credit receiver. The credit grantor is the seller, dealer, service provider, lessor, or a person who currently owns the rights of one of these parties. A credit receiver is the purchaser, a person to whom a service is rendered, a lessee, or a person to whom the rights of one of these parties have passed.

The text of Section 13 of the *Credit Agreements Act*, which entitles the credit receiver to terminate the contract under certain circumstances, must appear in the agreement. In an instalment sale transaction, the agreement must state the conditions of the passing of ownership or the right to the return of the goods.

Prohibited terms

Certain terms are not allowed in credit agreements. Provisions that exclude the protection of the parties or provisions that are regarded as generally unfair may not be included. If an agreement contains exclusions or generally unfair provisions, only the exclusion or unfair provision will become invalid and not the whole agreement.

The list of these prohibited terms and/or provisions is lengthy and complex. If you are planning to draw up any form of credit agreement, make sure you obtain professional legal advice.

The specific rights and duties of the credit grantor and credit receiver

The rights and duties of the parties to a credit agreement will be determined by the type of the contract; that is, whether it is a contract of sale, lease, or employment, and also by the terms of the agreement. In addition to the normal rights and duties, the *Credit Agreements Act* creates certain special rights and duties. A credit receiver cannot waive any right he or she has under the Act. The following are two basic rights of a credit receiver – that is, a purchaser – with regard to the repossession of goods bought on credit:

- **The credit receiver's right to a default notice before repossession:** If the credit receiver or the purchaser defaults on payment, the credit grantor may not repossess the goods until he or she has, by means of a registered or hand-delivered letter, notified the credit receiver of the breach and demanded compliance within the period fixed by the letter, allowing at least 30 days after the date of the handing over or posting of the letter. If the credit receiver fails to comply with his or her obligations within this period, the credit grantor may repossess the goods.

- **The credit receiver's right to reinstatement after repossession:** The credit receiver is entitled to have repossessed goods returned if, within 30 days of the repossession, he or she pays the amount due in terms of the agreement as well as the reasonable costs incurred by the credit grantor in connection with the repossession of the goods.

The deposit

The initial payment or deposit is very important in the context of the legislation, and various provisions are aimed at ensuring that the deposit is actually paid by the credit receiver.

A credit agreement does not become binding until the deposit has been paid – either in cash or in goods. If goods (for example, a motor vehicle) are traded in as a deposit, only their reasonable value will be regarded as payment on the deposit. The deposit may not be paid by way of a post-dated cheque or other post-dated negotiable instruments.

> The credit grantor or anyone acting on his or her behalf may not extend credit for the deposit or make money available to the credit receiver to enable him or her to pay the deposit

The maximum period

A credit agreement may not exceed the maximum period prescribed by the minister and provided for under the Act. The credit receiver is thus discouraged from concluding an agreement if the instalments necessary to discharge the full contract price within the maximum period are not affordable. If the period of a credit agreement is not stated, the agreement will automatically become invalid.

8.6 Lease agreements

Many small businesses rent their premises from a landlord who is the legal owner of the property. If you intend renting property, you should know your basic rights as a tenant. If, on the other hand, you are letting property to others, you will also need to have an understanding of what is expected of you as a lessor.

The lease granted by a landlord gives the tenants exclusive possession of the premises for a fixed period of time. At the end of this period, the property reverts back to the landlord. The tenants will normally be answerable to the landlord for the use of the property, and specific restrictions are normally agreed on and contained in the lease agreement.

The legal relationship between the lessor and the lessee may fall within the ambit of the *Rental Housing Act, 21 of 1999* (RHA).

South African law recognises three forms of the contract of letting and hiring. There is the letting and hiring of a movable or immovable item, the letting and hiring of services, and the letting and hiring of work to be done (for example, a house to be built). The following section deals mainly with the letting and hiring of immovable property, including a building or part thereof. It deals primarily with what is termed a contract of landlord and tenant.

> **Lease agreements:** A contract for the lease, or a contract for the letting and hiring of an item, is a reciprocal contract in terms of which one party (the lessor, or landlord) undertakes to make temporarily available to another party (the lessee, or tenant) the use and enjoyment of the item, wholly or in part, in return for the payment of a sum of money.

8.6.1 The essentials of a contract of lease

A contract of lease has three essential elements:

- an undertaking by the lessor to give the lessee the use and enjoyment of the item,
- an agreement between the lessor and the lessee that the lessee's use and enjoyment is to be temporary, and

- an undertaking to pay rent; in other words, the lessee agrees to pay a specific sum of money in return for the use and enjoyment that he or she will receive.

In principle, any corporeal or material or physical item, movable or immovable, can be let. It is not required that the contract should grant the full use and enjoyment of the item. A partial letting and hiring is allowed; for example, an office or workshop in a building may be let. The parties must therefore agree on the object that is to be the subject of the lease. The item, or part of it, that is let must be identified or identifiable.

A lease does not have to cover a specific period of time. It is up to the parties to decide, and they may agree to give a specific period of notice to end the rental agreement.

8.6.2 The rent

The lessee must undertake to pay rent. The rent must be in the form of money.

The amount of rent that is payable must be definite. Parties to a lease agreement normally agree on a specific amount of money, but they can also create a valid lease by agreeing to a method or formula by which the amount of rent is to be calculated.

8.6.3 Deposit

As far as a deposit is concerned, it is not a requirement of the contract. However, the parties usually agree on a deposit to be used by the lessor, if necessary, to cover arrear rental, the replacement of lost items, or any damage that may have been caused by the lessee.

The landlord must invest the deposit in an interest-bearing account with a financial institution, and interest will go to the tenant. The tenant may request the landlord to provide him or her with written proof concerning accrued interest over the lease period.

8.6.4 Inspections

The *Rental Housing Act* compels both the lessor and lessee to undertake a minimum of two joint inspections of the premises. The first one must take place prior to the tenant moving into the premises, as this particular inspection is to determine that the premises are in sound condition.

The second inspection must take place at the end of the lease period to determine whether there is any damage caused by the tenant during the period of the lease.

A lessor's or landlord's failure to inspect the premises in the presence of the lessee at the end of the lease period is taken as acknowledgement by the lessor that the premises have been returned in a good and acceptable state of repair.

In such cases, the lessor does not have the right to retain the deposit or any part of the deposit. If deductions are made from the deposit, receipts indicating the reasons for these deductions must be available to the tenant for inspection.

8.6.5 The formation of a contract of lease

No formalities are required for a valid contract of lease to come into effect. A lease, including a lease of land, may be informal. However, the *Rental Housing Act* states that a landlord must, if requested by a tenant, put a lease in writing. If you intend leasing a property for your business, ensure that a comprehensive document is drawn up between yourself and the landlord. Make certain that your legal advisor approves of the contents of the document before signing.

8.6.6 The rights and duties of the lessor and the lessee

Contracts of lease are often contained in standard-form contracts. The lessor and lessee may not exclude any of the essential elements of this type of contract. They must, for example, specify an object that is to be the subject of the lease, as well as the rent that will be payable.

However, they may exclude some consequences of the contract of lease that would otherwise have been covered by common law. The following paragraphs set out the position according to common law in the absence of any contrary contractual terms or provisions contained in the contract of lease.

8.6.7 The duties of the lessor

If you are letting any movable or immovable property, you must be aware that the lessor or owner of an item has certain duties under the law with regard to the letting of that item:

- **The duty to deliver the physical or material item let to the lessee:** The lessor must deliver the physical or material item to be let in a condition that will enable the lessee to use and enjoy it. Accessories that are essential to the proper use of the physical item (for example, the keys to the property), must be made available to the lessee.

- **The duty to maintain the physical or material item let in proper condition:** The physical or material item to be let must not only be delivered in good condition but must also be maintained in that state. The lessor must, allowing for normal wear and tear, maintain the item in the condition in which he or she was obliged to deliver it.

- **The duty to ensure the lessee's undisturbed use and enjoyment:** The lessor warrants that no one has the right to disturb the lessee's use and enjoyment of the property.

8.6.8 The duties of the lessee

If you are renting premises, vehicles, equipment, or other items, it is important to know that, in turn, the person leasing the property or item has certain duties in law. These include the following:

- **The lessee's duty to pay the rent:** The amount and time of payment of the rent are stipulated in the lease agreement and the lessee must pay this as per the agreement.

- **The lessor's tacit hypothec for unpaid rent (security):** If the lessee does not pay the rent as agreed, the lessor has a right over all movables situated on the property. This serves as security in respect of the rent. However, this only comes into effect when and for as long as the rent is in arrears. The lessor should seek legal advice before randomly attaching the lessee's moveables.

- **The lessee's duty of proper use and care of the thing let:** The lessee may not use the leased item improperly or unreasonably. The leased item must be maintained in good condition and may only be used for the purpose for which it has been leased.

- **The lessee's duty to restore the property or item let on termination of the lease:** Upon termination of the lease, the lessee must return the property or item and/or evacuate the premises. The property or item must be returned in the condition in which it was received, although deterioration as a result of reasonable wear and tear is accepted.

Should the property or item let be damaged or have been destroyed, the lessee is obliged to make good the damage unless he or she can show that the damage was not their fault – not caused either directly or indirectly by his or her employees, family, or other parties.

The rights of the lessor:

- The most important right of the lessor is the right to payment of the rent.
- The lessor also has the right, upon termination of the lease, to regain full control of the property in a good state of repair, save for fair wear and tear.
- If the property is damaged, the lessor is entitled to compensation.
- The lessor also has the right to demand that the lessee use the premises only for the purpose for which they were let and in the manner in which the premises would be used if the lessee were the premises' owner.
- The lessor also has the right to terminate the lease under certain circumstances.

The rights of the lessee:

- The most important right of the lessee is the right to the use and enjoyment of the leased premises.
- While doing so, the RHA confirms that the lessee, members of their household, and their visitors have the right to privacy that includes the right not to have their person, property, or the premises searched by the lessor.
- In this regard, the lessor only has a right of inspection performed in a reasonable manner after reasonable notice has been given to the lessee.
- The lessee also has the right to demand that the lessor maintains the leased premises in good condition unless agreed otherwise.

Subletting

Unless otherwise stipulated in the lease agreement, the lessee is entitled to sublet the property to a third party. This is done by means of a contract of sub-lease entered into between the lessee of the property and another party. In terms of the sub-lease, the normal relationship of lessor and lessee is established between the original lessee and the sub-lessee. The relationship between the original lessor and lessee remains unaffected and no rights and duties are constituted between the original lessor and the sub-lessee. The original lessor can, however, evict the sub-lessee if he or she stays in occupation of the premises after the original lease has terminated.

What happens if you are renting and the lessor sells the property?

'Hire takes precedence over sale' is the legal protection for tenants. This saying refers to the principle that the person to whom such property has been sold is bound by any contract of lease existing in respect of the property at the time of its sale. The purchaser therefore cannot evict the tenant but is obliged to abide by the terms of the lease, provided that the tenant continues to pay the rent due under the lease.

8.6.9 The termination of a lease

There are various ways of terminating a lease agreement:

- **Termination by passage of time:** If a lease is for a fixed period, the obligations arising from it automatically come to an end when the period ends.

- **Termination by notice:** If the contract of letting and hiring is for an indefinite period, but with rent payable periodically (for example, monthly), the agreement can be terminated by notice given by the lessor or the lessee to the other party. If there is no agreement on the period for such notice, reasonable notice must be given.

- **Termination by death:** This occurs when a lease is terminated by the death of the lessor or the lessee if the contract stipulates this.

8.6.10 The lessee's right to compensation for improvements

Improvements can be

- useful (if they improve the property and increase its market value),
- luxurious (if they satisfy the fancy of an individual, whether or not they increase the market value), and
- necessary (if they are required for the preservation of the property).

It is important that the parties to a rental contract should agree on the rights of the lessee to remove any improvements he or she has made to the property over the period of the lease. The parties should also agree on a lessee's right to claim compensation if improvements are not removed. If they have not agreed otherwise, the lessee may remove annexures constituting luxurious or useful improvements before the lease terminates, provided that the property will not be left in a worse condition than when it was received. After termination, everything annexed belongs to the lessor.

This is important when considering the cost and value of shop fittings or specialised equipment installed in a production environment such as a factory. To be safe, make sure that the lease agreement allows you to take any such fittings with you when you move.

8.6.11 Renewal of a lease

A contract of lease may be renewed immediately upon the expiration of the existing lease.

1. Define the following

   • lease,

   • rent,

   • lessor,

   • lessee, and

   • lease termination.

2. How would a lease be terminated?

3. What types of object or thing can be leased?

4. In your own business, what kinds of lease are you likely to enter into, and for what items?

8.7 Insurance agreements

Insurance is a contract between an insurance company (the insurer) and a person (the insured) whereby the insurer agrees, in return for the payment of a premium, to pay the insured a sum of money, or its equivalent, on the happening of an uncertain event in which the insured has some interest.

It is not a specific legal or statutory requirement in South Africa that you take out insurance to cover your business and its operation. However, many small businesses end up closing down or going into liquidation as a result of an unfortunate accident, theft, fire, public liability claim, or similar unforeseen occurrence. In 90 per cent of the cases, the owner or partners could so easily have taken out insurance that would have covered the event and allowed the business to continue.

Business insurance is one of the most critical and often most neglected aspects of ensuring your business's prosperity and sustainability. Many small business owners will have invested their life savings or will have been required to take out significant loans in order to finance the operation. Any single unforeseen event, such as a fire, robbery, or injury, or an accident to a customer, can cripple that business overnight.

Whatever you do, don't underestimate the need for insurance. For example, what if there is a fire on the farm and Jaque loses her building, equipment, and stock? If she is properly insured, she will be compensated by the insurer, and will be able to get the business going again. If not, it could mean the end of the business.

> Some may say that they cannot afford to insure their business, but most in the know will say that you cannot afford *not* to insure your business.

8.7.1 Who is required to take out insurance?

Anyone currently running a business or intending to open up a business should take out insurance to protect their investment. Every business is different and will therefore have its own unique needs and requirements when it comes to insurance. Remember, your insurance premiums will depend on the type of business you own, the history and liabilities of the business, and the range of services you offer.

Invariably, if you make application for a loan from a financial institution, you will be required to take out some form of personal insurance as collateral. If, for example, you buy a vehicle on hire purchase or buy land or a building on a bond basis, you will be required to take out some form of insurance.

But, over and above loan insurance, you must also consider coverage against accidents involving members of the public and their goods, your employees, yourself, and your property. You will need to look into such matters as all risks, buildings and content cover, employer's liability, public liability, vehicles, goods in transit, business interruption and legal expenses, equipment (breakdown and loss of licence), machinery, tools, and signs, and fidelity guarantee.

You should discuss all of the possible insurance options available with an insurance company, broker, or agent as soon as you start up your business or, better still, even before you open the doors.

8.7.2 Who will I be dealing with?

Getting the correct business insurance cover to protect your small business venture will take some time and you will need to shop around for the most suitable insurance company or broker. Today, an increasing number of insurance companies, brokers, and agents are setting up comprehensive small business insurance packages. There are a number of ways of finding out who best to deal with.

- Talk to other business owners or associates who have a similar business and find out who they are using and whether they recommend you contact them.

- If you already have personal insurance and you are happy with the insurance company or broker you are dealing with, contact them and find out whether they offer comprehensive small business insurance packages. If they cannot offer the service you are looking for, find out who they would recommend you contact.

- Try to find an insurance company or broker who is familiar with your industry and your type of business.

- Contact the trade associations that occur in your industry and ascertain whether they have an agreement with anyone or can recommend a reputable company or broker.

No matter what you decide or who you decide to insure with, make sure that you sign up with a reputable and financially sound insurance company. You are looking for a company that offers the right package at the right price and that can handle and pay out bone-fide claims quickly. Waiting for a couple of weeks, against waiting a couple of months, can make the difference between survival and disaster.

Look for a company that is open and honest about the so-called 'small print' – all those clauses contained in your insurance agreement, written in legal jargon, that are almost impossible to understand. These are the ones that you are reminded of only after your claim has been rejected.

8.7.3 What should be insured?

First and foremost, as with most other aspects of your business, you will be looking to get the best possible and most comprehensive small business insurance package, at the lowest possible cost. Comprehensive coverage is obviously very important, but, at the same time, it will need to be balanced with what the business can afford.

There are many different forms of insurance that could apply or be beneficial to your business. Examples of the types of insurance that should be discussed with the insurance company or broker are listed below. The list is by no means exhaustive, but it will give you a good idea about what you and your insurance representative should be discussing.

- **Public liability insurance:** This will protect your business from financial loss as a result of an injury, death, or property damage caused by business operations, employees, or products to a client or customer. This is particularly important for any businesses that may have any risk to do with the public, such as if you are serving members of the public in your shop, if you operate any adventure activities, if you provide food for public consumption, and so on. This covers property of guests or customers on your property, and also insures you if anything happens to them when on your property – such as if they slip on a wet floor and injure themselves. This should also cover any possible damage to a guest or customer's property by an employee – for example, if you are running a leather repair shop and one of your staff accidentally damages a leather handbag belonging to a customer, insurance should cover you for such incidents.

- **Building and property:** This provides coverage against any form of damage, whether it is by fire, vandalism, or any other cause.

- **Contents – office and assets:** This covers the loss of the content of your business which may occur as a result of fire, vandalism, or any other cause.

- **Burglary or theft:** Not only do you need to protect your own business against theft or robbery, but you would be wise to cover possible guest or client losses, especially if you are planning to open an accommodation establishment.

- **Business disruption or loss of income:** If, for some reason beyond your control, you are no longer able to operate for a period of time, such as a result of a fire, you should consider protecting this potential loss of income.

- **Cash:** If you handle a significant amount of cash in your business, you should consider coverage.

- **Debtors:** If you have a high level of debtors (people who owe you money), it would certainly be an idea to cover any potential loss as a result of non-payment.

- **Embezzlement or unlawful appropriation of goods:** You can insure yourself against the loss of goods, products, and money as a result of unlawful actions by your employees.

- **Fire:** The risk of fire varies from one industry to another. For example, accommodation establishments and restaurants run a relatively high fire risk and should therefore be covered.

- **Goods in transit:** If you are required to transport products and goods, you could look to protect your business against any loss as a result of theft or accidents.

- **Personal accident and life:** By taking out a life or accident insurance policy, you will be protecting your business against the death or injury of key personnel, including yourself. You will need to consider protecting your family or your partners in the business.

- **Vehicle and passenger liability cover:** Not only must you insure your vehicle(s) but, if you intend transporting paying or even non-paying clients and customers, you should be looking at some form of insurance to protect you and your business against any potential claim as a result of an accident resulting in injury or death.

Evaluate the existing insurance that you have taken out on your property, business, or life. Identify all your business processes and likely business risks. Compare this to the list above and determine whether you have sufficient insurance to cover you in all eventualities.

8.7.4 Legal aspects of insurance

Business owners must be careful about whom they deal with when purchasing any form of insurance. Brokers, for example, should preferably be members of professional insurance associations such as the Insurance Brokers Council (IBC) or the South African Insurance Brokers Association (SAIBA). Members of these institutions are obliged to insure themselves against professional negligence, which, in turn, gives the insured party protection in the case of negligence or misconduct on the part of the broker. These institutions are bound by a strict code of ethics.

Disclaimers

The impact of the cost of insurance premiums can be reduced if the establishment uses proper disclaimers, which are approved by insurers.

Disclaimers can take various forms and usually appear in notices at swimming pools and parking areas. Make sure that your legal advisor draws up any of the disclaimers you intend using.

It is also very important to bring the contents of a disclaimer to your customers' attention. This may be achieved by incorporating properly drafted wording on forms, invoices, receipts, and so on.

8.7.5 Insurance contracts

The contract is usually formed when a person or organisation completes a proposal form and submits it to an insurer for consideration. The contract is completed when the insurance company accepts the proposal unconditionally and when this is communicated to the insured.

There must be agreement on all the terms of the contract. These terms include:

- the person or property to be insured,
- the risk that is being insured against,
- the amount payable on the occurrence of the event,
- the premium to be paid by the insured, and
- the period of cover.

Once the insurer agrees to insure, a document setting out the terms of the contract of insurance is issued. This is known as an insurance policy. The proposal form is an extremely important part of the insurance contract, as it forms the basis on which the insurer agreed to insure.

8.7.6 Types of insurance contract

The law recognises two types of insurance agreement, namely indemnity insurance and non-indemnity insurance contracts.

- **Indemnity insurance:** Indemnity insurance requires the insurer to undertake to make good the damage that the insured may have suffered through the occurrence of the particular event insured against. Common examples of indemnity insurance are fire, theft, and motor vehicle insurance. The insurer is obliged to compensate the insured for the actual loss that has been suffered, provided the insured is adequately covered. In this case, the insured is not compensated for consequences such as inconvenience and sentimental loss.

- **Non-indemnity insurance:** In the case of non-indemnity insurance, the insurer undertakes to pay the insured or the beneficiary a fixed sum of money if the event insured against takes place. Examples of non-indemnity insurance include life and personal accident insurance.

8.7.7 Essentialia of the insurance contract

The essentialia of a contract are those characteristics of a particular contract that distinguish it from other types of contract. In this regard, it is not easy to identify the essentialia of an insurance contract, as neither the courts nor the government have as yet provided a comprehensive definition.

An insurance contract usually contains the following:

- an undertaking by the insured to pay a premium,
- an undertaking by the insurer to pay a sum of money or its equivalent,
- a particular uncertain future event upon which the insurer's obligation to pay will depend (the risk), and
- an insurable interest.

The premium

The insured undertakes to pay a premium. The premium is usually a sum of money. Although the actual payment of the premium is not a requirement for the creation of the contract, payment is usually a condition for the policy to take effect.

An undertaking by the insurer to pay a sum of money

This undertaking is formed by the type of insurance agreement, as described below.

- **Determination of the amount payable (non-indemnity insurance):** In the case of non-indemnity insurance, the sum payable will be a predetermined amount. Where, for example, a person insures his or her life for R250 000 (the insured amount), the insurer will have to pay that amount to the estate of the insured or the beneficiary.
- **Determination of the amount payable (indemnity insurance):** In the case of indemnity insurance, the insurer's obligation is to pay a determinable sum of money. The exact amount of the payment is determined after the occurrence of the event insured against, by determining the extent of the damage.

For example, if a shop valued at R200 000 is insured against fire, and at the time it was destroyed by fire it is worth R250 000, then the insured's loss, which he or she may recover from the insurer, is R250 000. Normally, however, a maximum value of compensation is stipulated in the insurance contract.

Where the object has only been damaged, the insurer will be liable for the amount of the partial loss suffered. The extent of partial loss is usually taken to be the cost of repairing the risk object.

Other principles that are applicable to indemnity insurance contracts include the following:

- **The insurer's right to repair:** An insurer often reserves the right in an insurance contract to have the damaged risk object repaired, instead of compensating the insured.

- **Insuring with several insurers:** An insured has the right to insure the same risk object with as many insurers as he or she wishes. In the event of a loss occurring, the insured may, however, only recover the full amount of the loss and no more.

Over- and under-insurance

There is nothing to prevent someone from insuring for a larger amount than is necessary to secure full compensation in the event of the loss of the insured risk object. In the case of indemnity insurance, however, the insured may recover no more than the total value of the loss.

Where an insured insures for an amount less than the actual value of the insured object, he or she is under-insured. For example, if Helen's car, valued at R20 000, is insured for R12 000, and the car is damaged to the value of R10 000, Helen will be able to recover only R6 000 because, as she insured for only six-tenths of the value, she can recover only six-tenths of her loss.

Excess clauses

In motor vehicle and liability insurance, so-called excess clauses are common. In terms of these clauses, the insured must bear a specific proportion of the loss himself or herself, such as the first R1 000 of the loss.

The risk

The uncertain event insured against is known as the risk. Description of the risk in the contract is important, because the insurer must know precisely the nature of the risk, and the insured must know the extent of his or her cover. The parties always agree to insure against the occurrence of a specific (or determinable) event. The insurer's obligations are always coupled with some event that must cause the result mentioned in the contract, for example a fire that damages the insured's house.

The description of the risk must include

(a) the object insured, for example a motor car, or a person's life,

(b) the hazard insured against, for example theft, and

(c) the circumstances affecting the risk, for example limitation of the insurance to theft of a motor car while it is parked in a specific place.

It is very important for small business operators to ensure that their policies cover the risks that they wish to insure against. In this regard, exclusion and excess clauses are vitally important as insurers always limit their liability and an insurer will only accept liability for a loss that falls within the limits of the policy. For example, if you think you run a fire risk in your business, make sure that this is included in the contract in the risk section.

8.7.8 Insurance brokers

Apart from the insurer and the insured, other parties may also be involved when an insurance contract is concluded. These include insurance brokers who are independent people who arrange insurance contracts between their clients and insurers.

Brokers are not tied to any one particular insurer and are therefore not compelled to sell their products only. Brokers are in a position to recommend the best insurer, depending on their client's needs. An insurance broker is primarily the agent of an insured, and is mandated to obtain insurance coverage for him or her.

8.7.9 The insurer

The insurance industry is regulated by the *Long-term Insurance Act, 52 of 1998*, and the *Short-term Insurance Act, 53 of 1998*. This legislation aims at protecting the interests of those who invest in the insurance industry. It stipulates that only companies registered in accordance with the Acts are entitled to carry on the business of insurance.

8.7.10 The insured

It is a basic requirement of a valid insurance contract that the insured must have an insurable interest in the subject matter of the insurance. This is because insurance is about compensation for loss, and it is only when a person has an insurable interest that he or she will suffer loss when the risk insured against occurs.

1. Define the following

   - risk,

   - insured,

   - insurer,

   - broker,

   - indemnity insurance,

   - non-indemnity insurance, and

   - short-term insurance.

2. Write a short article for a business newsletter on the reasons for and the advantage of insurance.

3. What should you be cautious about when taking out insurance?

4. In your own business, what kind of insurance will you need to protect yourself?

8.8 Employment contracts

If you intend employing people for your business, it is more often than not obligatory for you to provide an employment contract that will govern the relationship between both parties. This will provide protection for both you and your employees.

In Jaque's case, she will probably employ people to help her in preparing the fruit (peeling and chopping), and then cooking and bottling. She may also need help to pack cases of bottles and to deliver or ship them to her clients. She will need to formalise the employment contracts in writing to protect herself and her staff.

This section will outline the essentialia of the contract and discuss the various aspects and legal requirements of employment contracts.

The **contract of employment** can be defined as an agreement between two parties, in terms of which one party (the employee or worker) places his or her labour potential at the disposal of and under the control of the other party (the employer), in exchange for some form of remuneration.

From this definition, it is clear that the essentialia of the contract of employment will be the provision of work and the subsequent remuneration or pay. The contract is reciprocal in nature: the employee provides his or her labour in return for remuneration from the employer. A distinguishing feature of the employment relationship is the element of subordination and control. The employer generally has the right to control the employee, and the relationship is essentially one of inequality. The employer generally has greater bargaining power, unless the employees increase their power by forming and joining trade unions and bargaining collectively with the employer.

> The **parties to an employment contract:** There must be two parties to a contract of employment – the employer and the employee.
>
> The **employer:** The employer may be a natural person or a juristic person, such as a company or a close corporation.
>
> The **employee:** The employee will always be a natural person.

There are certain statutory limitations on who may be employed. For example, the *Basic Conditions of Employment Act (BCEA)* provides that no employer shall employ a person under the age of 15 years.

8.8.1 The duration of an employment contract

It is up to the parties to the employment contract to agree on the nature of their relationship and the duration of the contract. In this regard, it is possible to distinguish between indefinite employment contracts and fixed-term employment contracts.

Many employees are appointed on an indefinite (permanent) basis. In this case, termination of the employment contract is subject to the rules discussed below.

Sometimes, employees are appointed either for a specific period or to perform a specific task. In these cases, the contract of employment terminates automatically on completion of or expiry of the period or task.

8.8.2 The content of an employment contract

Typically, an employment contract will provide for a number of issues. These will include, but not necessarily be limited to,

- the job description of the employee,
- the hours of work (including possible overtime work, work on Sundays, and work on public holidays),

- the remuneration, and how and when it will be paid,
- the amount of leave (vacation, sick, maternity, and family responsibility leave) to which the employee will be entitled,
- whether the employer will pay for relocation expenses (if any),
- restraint of trade, and
- the duties of the employee in relation to the employer.

For the most part, employment contracts are rather brief – the parties simply include all the existing policies of the employer by reference in their contract. It is important to bear in mind that, although parties, as a general rule, can decide what to put in the contract, they are not entirely free to do so. This is as a result of two particular guiding principles.

First, certain aspects of common law are automatically part of the contract, unless specifically excluded. Second, legislation dictates and limits the freedom of the parties not only to decide on what rights and duties will be part of their contract (an employer, for example, will be required to give female employees maternity leave), but also what the level of certain rights in the contract should be (in terms of the *Basic Conditions of Employment Act*, an employer is required to give female employees four months' maternity leave).

An example of a template for a contract of employment is on the next page.

8.8.3 The duties of an employer

The employer has a number of duties towards the employee, which are set out in the *Basic Conditions of Employment Act*, as well as in other labour legislation.

To pay remuneration

Generally speaking, there is nothing in law that lays down how much an employee is to be paid. However, industry or company specific collective agreements and industry/sector specific Sectoral Determinations (in terms of the BCEA) may establish minimum wages and the parties will then be bound by contract to pay at least the minimum wage or more.

- **The 'no work, no pay' rule:** In terms of the common law, the general rule is 'no work, no pay'. If the worker has not performed in terms of the contract, the employer does not have to pay the employee.
- **Unjust enrichment:** If an employee has worked for part of a month and terminates the contract, the employer must generally pay for the services

organivan
farm fresh organically grown produce

PO Box 2543, Slabberts, 5300 • Tel: 058 298 3006 • Fax: 058 298 2738 • Email: organivan@maxitec.co.za

Contract of employment

between

[Employer name]

and

[Employee name]

Strictly confidential

Dear [Employee name]

We are pleased to be able to offer you a contract of employment with [employer name] effective from [date] in the capacity of [position]

1. Employment

Your employment with [employer name] is on a permanent/contract basis. You shall report to [manager name].

2. Duties and responsibilities

During your employment you shall:

Be

Comply with ....

Carry out ....

3. Other employment

While this agreement remains in force, you shall not be engaged or take part, directly or indirectly, whether as an employee or in any other capacity, in any other business without the [employer name] consent.

4. Remuneration

In return for services rendered in terms of this Agreement, you shall be paid a gross salary of R .... per month. This includes ....

Your salary, less deductions, shall be paid monthly in arrears on the 28th day of every month.

5. Medical Aid

[Employer name] subscribes to the [medical aid fund]. Membership is voluntary/ compulsory. Should you join, [employer name] will contribute x percentage of your monthly premium up to a maximum of R ....

6. Pension fund

[Employer name] subscribes to [pension fund]. The monthly contribution to the fund is 13%

of salary, of which 7% will be paid by [employer name] and the balance by the employee. Membership of the fund is compulsory/voluntary.

7. Place of work

Your place of work will be [physical address of work]

8. Working hours

The ordinary working hours of [employer name] are [state hours] from [Monday to Friday]. You are entitled to a daily lunch break of 30 minutes that can be taken at your convenience/at [specify time].

9. Overtime

You will be paid overtime in accordance with the stipulations in the Terms and Conditions of Employment attached hereto.

10. Performance management

Your performance will be managed in accordance with the stipulations in the Terms and Conditions of Employment attached hereto.

11. Leave

You are entitled to x working days' annual leave, to be taken in a 12-month period.

During every period of 36 consecutive months' employment, you are entitled to 30 days' paid sick leave. If you are absent from work due to illness, you must notify your manager of your absence by 09h00 on the first day of absence.

Other leave may be granted in terms of the Terms and Conditions of Employment attached hereto.

12. Termination

It is specifically recorded that this agreement may be terminated at any stage for misconduct, incapacity, poor performance, or operational requirements of [employer name], or for any reason justified in law.

Your employment may be terminated by you or by [employer] on giving one calendar month's notice in writing.

13. Deductions

By your signature to this contract, you authorise [employer], upon termination of your employment for any reason whatsoever, to deduct any amounts due by you to [employer name].

14. Conditions of employment

In your capacity as an employee of [employer name] all the [employer name] polices and procedures will apply to you and will form part of the Contract of Employment.

Yours faithfully,

CEO

Signed: [employee].. date:..

already rendered, based on the principle that one person may not be unjustly enriched at the expense of another. This principle may not apply if the employee has deserted the employer.

- **The payment of the remuneration:** Wages or salary are normally paid in cash, but may be partly paid in kind, by providing the employee with a benefit such as accommodation. It is important to note, however, that payment of remuneration will, in most instances, be governed by the *Basic Conditions of Employment Act*, collective agreements, or industry/sector-specific Sectoral Determinations.

To receive the employee into service

The employer must honour the contractual obligation to enter into the employment relationship with the employee.

However, the employer does not have a general duty to provide the employee with work, for as long as the employee is paid in terms of the contract. Exceptions to this rule include the situation where the employee is paid on commission and this commission depends on the provision of work; for example, where a salesperson relies on the employer to make business appointments.

To provide safe working conditions

The employer has a common law and statutory duty to provide the employee with safe working conditions, safe machinery, and safe tools. The *Occupational Health and Safety Act* also places further responsibility on the employer in this regard.

Not to victimise the employee

The *Labour Relations Act*, the BCEA, the *Employment Equity Act*, and the *Occupational Health and Safety Act, 85 of 1993* all contain provisions outlawing victimisation by an employer of an employee for exercising a constitutional or statutory right, such as that of freedom of association, or the right to strike.

Vicarious liability

An employer can be held liable by a third party for any unlawful act performed by its employees during the course and scope of their duties. Should you ever be in a position where the negligence of a staff member has caused a liability claim against your business, you should seek professional legal advice on the matter, as various prerequisites apply.

8.8.4 The duties of an employee

Although the employee has freedom to contract, the provisions of the common law play a significant role in setting out his or her duties.

To enter into the service of the employer

The primary duty of an employee is to actually place his or her labour potential at the disposal of the employer. In terms of the 'no work, no pay' rule, if the employee does not work, there is generally no entitlement to remuneration.

To work competently and without negligence

The employee implicitly guarantees that he or she is capable of doing the work for which he or she contracted. There is a further duty to exercise due care and diligence. A failure to perform the work competently and without negligence will result in a breach of contract and a possible termination of the employment relationship.

To obey all reasonable and lawful commands

The employee, as stated above, is under the control and authority of the employer. The employee, therefore, has an implied duty to obey all reasonable and lawful commands given by the employer. Serious insubordination may amount to a breach of contract.

To act in good faith

The common-law duty to act in good faith is implied in every contract of employment: it exists even if it is not an express term of the contract.

- **Confidential information:** The unauthorised use or divulging of confidential information amounts to a breach of good faith, if it occurs during or even after the period of employment has terminated. An employee is entitled to use general knowledge acquired during employment, but not knowledge that is confidential in nature. The distinction between the two may not always be easy to make.

- **The employee must promote the business of the employer:** The employee must devote his or her hours of work to furthering the employer's business. The employee may not, therefore, work for another employer if there is a conflict of interest with the original employer.

- **The employee may not compete with the employer:** For example, by providing the same product or service in his or her own time for his or her own profit.

- **The employee must act honestly:** Any dishonest behaviour on the part of an employee, such as theft, fraud, or the procurement of secret commissions (kickbacks), will be a breach of good faith. If the breach is serious, the employer may summarily dismiss the employee.

8.8.5 Termination of the contract of employment

Some of the most common ways in which a contract of employment may be lawfully terminated are briefly discussed below:

- **Termination on completion of the agreed period or task:** A contract of employment is often concluded for an indefinite period and may be terminated lawfully by giving the required notice. Sometimes, a contract of employment, called a 'fixed-term contract' is for a specified period or for the completion of a certain project. This particular contract will usually state expressly that it is for a fixed term, but in some cases this may be implied. Normally, the fixed-term contract expires automatically and no notice need be given to effect its termination. The contract may, however, be expressly or implicitly renewed.

- **Termination by mutual agreement of the parties:** Not only should the parties agree to the contents of the agreement prior to the contract coming into existence, they may also agree to mutual termination of the contract. The agreement must, however, be mutual and it must be freely given.

- **Termination by notice:** A contract of service for an indefinite period may be terminated by one party giving the other notice of intention to terminate the contract. The period of notice is usually stipulated in the contract. It is important to note that the BCEA sets out statutory minimum notice periods. If the contract does not specify the notice period, the period of notice will be that provided for by the BCEA.

- **Termination on grounds of impossibility of performance:** If one of the parties is no longer able to perform in terms of the contract, for a period that is considered to be unreasonable, the other party is generally entitled to terminate the contract in terms of common law, unless the non-performance is caused by a party to the contract.

- **Termination on insolvency:** Although not covered in terms of common law, it is important to note that the *Insolvency Act, 24 of 1936* provides that the contract of employment of all employees will terminate automatically on the sequestration or liquidation of the employer. The employees will be entitled to claim unpaid wages, leave pay, and bonuses from the insolvent estate. The insolvency of the employee, on the other hand, does not generally affect the employment contract.

1. Where will you find the basic conditions of employment as laid down by the government?

2. On what grounds may employment be terminated?

3. Draw up a draft letter/contract of employment that you can use in your own business. This should include your own conditions of work, company name, and so on.

4. Who are the parties to an employment contract, and who governs such a contract?

8.9 Franchises

Franchises are an accepted form of business for persons wishing to use an existing successful and proven business model to create their own sustainable income. There are many different types of franchise available across all sectors of industry. These range from health care, bin cleaning, estate agencies, bead shops, stationers, and printers to restaurants and fast-food outlets.

The level of investment and capital needed will vary hugely from around R50 000 to many millions for a large and equipment-intensive franchise.

The term **franchise** refers to a situation in which a person who has developed a complete (and successful) business package grants another person the right to use that package in exchange for the payment of royalties. The person who grants the right to use his or her business package is the *franchiser*, and the person who pays for it is the *franchisee*.

When deciding on a franchise, the franchisee has to accept that he or she will have to run the business according to the franchiser's business model. The franchisee uses the franchiser's marketing strategy to attract and keep customers. The franchisee receives the right to use the franchiser's trademark, logo, trade name, and advertising. Franchising allows a number of businesses to use the same brand identification.

Under a franchise agreement, the franchiser grants the right to the franchisee to sell an agreed product or service in a particular geographical location. If, for example, the business is a fast-food outlet, the franchiser will limit or exclude other similar franchised fast-food outlets from opening up within a certain distance of the premises.

Advantages

The franchisee gains the following advantages from a successful franchise:

- The franchiser provides training and ongoing support and as a result the franchisee need not necessarily require previous experience.
- All the information and training that is needed for setting up and running the franchise is provided by the franchiser.
- The franchisee receives a complete operating manual on how to manage the business.
- The business format has been tried and tested. Teething problems normally encountered in starting a business have been overcome and, as a result, a franchise is usually up and running sooner than a completely new business. The franchisee inevitably experiences success sooner.
- It is a proven way of doing business, although it is not a guarantee of success.
- Because of the scale of the business, the franchiser has considerable negotiating power with product and service suppliers. The benefits of these cost savings can be passed on to the franchisee.
- The franchisee develops a customer base faster.
- The franchiser usually undertakes continued product development and research, which is made available to the franchisee.
- Franchising provides the franchiser a continuous supply of income through royalties paid by the franchisee.

Disadvantages

The following are disadvantages that affect the franchisee:

- An initial fee is payable to the franchiser, as well as a percentage of the annual profits.
- Set-up and capital costs are dictated by the franchise requirements.
- The franchiser controls and therefore limits the scope of the franchise and the operational business methods to be implemented.

- The franchiser may be the sole supplier of stock to the business, which possibly limits the scope of the franchisee to find more competitive suppliers.
- The sale of the franchise may not always be easy.

8.9.1 Franchise agreements

Franchisers are obliged, by a code of ethics, to provide all prospective franchisees with a disclosure document and a copy of the franchise agreement. After the franchisee agreement has been signed, there is an automatic seven-day cooling-off period. During this period, the potential franchisee is given an opportunity to further consider the proposal and, should he or she wish to back out of the agreement, they may do so without being in breach of the contract of franchise.

A franchise comes into being through a contract of franchise being agreed between the franchiser and the franchisee. A franchise agreement will contain clauses covering the following aspects of the business:

- the business name and the use to which the name can be put,
- the territory within which the franchisee can operate,
- the period of time for which the franchise is granted,
- the initial fee to be paid by the franchisee for the franchise, the service fee, and the advertising levy,
- the limitations on the scope of the business, including the franchisee's right to sell or transfer the franchise, and
- terms that put the agreement into effect, including sales targets, the purchase of supplies from the franchiser, quality control, training and franchise support, and management and advisory services.

Although the contracts offered by the various franchise organisations may differ, many of them will contain certain common terminology. Franchise contracts are usually standard-form contracts that leave little room for negotiation. The reason for this is that successful franchise networks require brand uniformity across every aspect of the business. The franchise contract is thus used as a tool to enforce these requirements. It places obligations on both parties to their mutual advantage.

8.9.2 The duties of the franchiser

The franchiser is obliged to

- disclose the business system to the franchisee,
- make available the intellectual property licensed to the franchisee in terms of the franchise agreement, and
- advise the franchisee on matters relating to the establishment of the franchised business, such as
  - suitable premises,
  - the design and decor of the premises,
  - shop fittings and electrical wiring,
  - sign writing,
  - sources of supply for equipment and furnishings, and
  - other requirements specifically related to the particular franchise.

The franchiser usually provides the franchisee with training. The franchiser determines, in consultation with the franchisee, which of the franchisee's employees will undergo training. The franchiser must provide or supply the franchisee with the same services and facilities that the franchiser supplies or provides to its other franchisees.

The franchise contract will oblige the franchiser to provide on-going support services after the conclusion of the contract. These services will include

- marketing and advertising,
- the development of the business systems to meet the changing demands of commerce,
- advice and training, and
- the disclosure of all improvements and developments in the business system and, as a result, to provide further training to the franchisee.

8.9.3 The duties of the franchisee

The franchisee is obliged to conduct the business strictly according to the operations manual. The franchisee also undertakes to meet any requirements that the franchiser may issue from time to time. These may be, for example, special offers, changes to an operating standard, or new products.

The franchisee and/or his or her employees are obliged to undergo training by the franchiser. The franchisee may not induce employees of fellow franchisees to leave their current place of employment.

The franchised business is usually conducted from premises that were approved by the franchiser. The premises must be maintained in a good and clean condition. The franchiser may require the franchisee to redecorate or refurbish the premises to ensure that the premises are in the same condition as those of other franchisees. The franchisee is also required to observe minimum business hours.

The franchisee is not permitted to advertise or conduct promotional marketing activities without the prior written approval of the franchiser. The franchisee is, however, obliged to use and display the franchiser's point-of-sale advertising or promotional material.

The franchisee is obliged to allow the franchiser access to the premises at reasonable times in order to carry out inspections or investigations that may be considered necessary for the purposes of ascertaining whether or not the provisions of the agreement between the parties are being complied with.

8.9.4 The protection of the franchiser's intellectual property

A franchisee obtains a right or licence to use the intellectual property of the franchiser, but does not become the owner of the intellectual property. The franchisee may not do anything, or cause, or permit anything to occur, that may adversely affect the franchiser's rights to the intellectual property.

The franchisee not only obtains the right to use the franchiser's trademarks but is obliged to do so. The franchisee does not, however, become the owner of the trademarks. The use of a well-known and distinctive trademark obviously benefits the franchisee. To maintain the distinctiveness of the trademark, the franchisee is obliged, when using the trademark, to reproduce it exactly and accurately and in accordance with specifications and directions laid down by the franchiser from time to time.

The franchisee may not divulge nor allow to be divulged, to any person, any aspect of the business systems, the know-how, or the trade secrets other than for any purpose as laid down in the franchise agreement. In this regard, the franchisee and his or her employees may be required to sign a confidentiality undertaking.

8.9.5 Restraints of trade on the franchisee and the franchiser

The maintenance of standards, protection of the brand, and need for uniformity will result in the franchise agreement containing certain restraints of trade. The franchisee may, for example, be obliged to restrict the operation of the business to certain premises or a specified geographical location. There may also be price restraints in terms of which the franchisee is obliged to supply the franchise products or services at a prescribed price to the public.

The franchiser may place a restraint on the franchisee with regard to the purchase of certain products. The franchisee may, for example, be obliged to buy specific supplies or products direct from the franchiser or from suppliers nominated by the franchiser.

Another restraint of trade may cover such matters as the franchisee not being permitted to have an interest in any other business that competes directly with the franchised business, during the term of the franchise agreement or for a certain period of time after its termination.

Restraints of trade are also placed on the franchiser. The purpose of the restraint is usually to offer the franchisee some form of protection against additional competition. If the franchisee is granted an exclusive location, the franchiser may be obliged not to operate or grant any other person the right to a similar franchise within that specified area.

8.9.6 Payment obligations

The franchisee usually pays the franchiser an initial lump sum once the contract has been finalised and the seven-day cooling off period has expired. Thereafter, royalties are usually paid throughout the period of the contract. The royalties may be fixed amounts that are payable periodically, or may be calculated as a percentage of turnover or sales within a set period of time such as a month, a quarter, or a year.

The lump-sum payment is usually an initial payment for the rights granted in terms of the agreement and for the equipment, advice, assistance, and training provided by the franchiser in terms of the agreement to enable the franchisee to establish the business.

In addition to the royalties, the franchise agreement may also provide for additional levies related to specific services by the franchiser. The franchisee may, for example, be obliged to pay the franchiser an amount for marketing or advertising campaigns, which are more often than not calculated as a percentage of the net sales.

8.9.7 Termination of the agreement

Franchise agreements may provide for the termination of the contract after a fixed period or on the death, insolvency, or incapacity of the franchisee. The contract may provide that, on the death of the franchisee, the franchiser may approve the transfer of the business to any of the beneficiaries of the deceased.

Upon termination of the agreement, the franchisee must immediately cease from any further use of the trademarks and of any other intellectual property that was licensed to him or her. The franchisee must hand over all dies, blocks, labels, advertising material, and printed matter featuring the trademarks.

8.10 Self-evaluation

1. Sandile and Sean are looking to establish their own business in the seaside town of Knysna. They are considering buying a franchise. Draw a flowchart that will help them understand how to go about applying for a franchise, from the initial contact with the franchiser to the setting up and opening of the business.

2. Define the following:
   - franchise,
   - franchisor,
   - franchisee, and
   - restraint of trade.

3. What are the benefits of buying a franchise?

4. What are the benefits of setting up your own franchise? What would the process be?

5. As an entrepreneur, what are the disadvantages of buying a franchise?

6. Go onto the Internet and find out where you can obtain guidance and advice on franchising – either to buy a franchise or to develop one.

9 Conditions of employment

9.1 Learning outcomes

After you have studied this chapter, you should be able to

- describe the foundation of labour legislation in South Africa,

- identify the contents of the *Labour Relations Act*,

- Identify which employment conditions apply to your business,

- apply the *Basic Conditions of Employment Act* to your employees if applicable,

- apply a Bargaining Council agreement to your business if applicable,

- apply a Sectoral Determination agreement to your business if applicable,

- draw up various employment forms, and

- access and use codes of good practice where relevant to your business.

9.2 Introduction

South Africa's system of labour relations revolves around various rules, processes, structures, and procedures that are used by the state, business, trade unions, employers, and employees to manage the relationship within the workplace.

The government supports freedom of association and collective bargaining as a fundamental and integral part of its labour relations strategy. A series of labour legislation has been published by the government over the years with the primary objective of setting parameters for the conduct of the relationship in the workplace and to ensure the protection of both employers and employees.

Chapter 3 of the South African Constitution sets out certain fundamental rights for all citizens of the country and makes the content of the chapter binding on all legislative and executive organs of the state at all levels of government. This means that all forms of South African legislation, at the national, provincial and local levels, must give rise to and support these principles, and that no law may contain any provision which is contrary to these rights:

- Every person shall have the right to fair labour practices.
- Employees shall have the right to form and join trade unions.
- Employers shall have the right to form and join employer associations.
- Employers and employees shall have the right to organise and bargain collectively.
- Employees shall have the right to strike for the purposes of collective bargaining.
- Employers shall have the right of 'lock-out' for the purposes of collective bargaining.

As a direct result, the official labour relations policy of the government of South Africa is based on the following principles:

- the right to work,
- the right to fair remuneration and conditions of service,
- the right of access to training and retraining,
- the right to organise and belong to a trade union,
- the right to bargain and negotiate collectively,
- the right to protection of safety and health,
- the right to security against unemployment,
- the right to security in the event of injury at work, and
- the right to job security and protection against unfair labour practices.

In order to give rise to all of the labour principles adopted by the government, the Department of Labour has, over the last eight to ten years, introduced a significant number of new and amended labour legislative Acts and regulations.

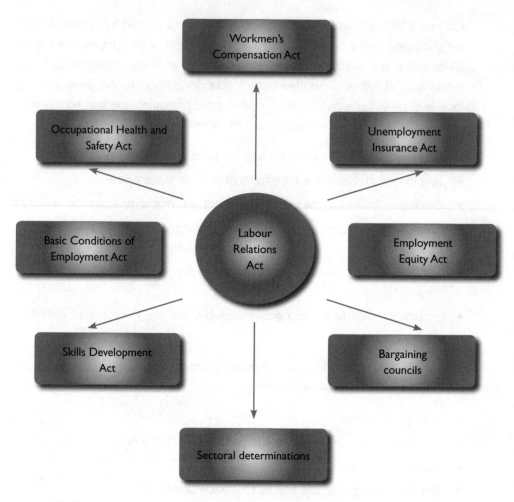

In effect, South African labour law revolves around the Labour Relations Act. The various labour enactments, as indicated in the diagram above, give rise to the key policies adopted by the Department of Labour, which are as follows:

- to leave the regulation of labour relations to employers and employees as far as is possible,

- to legislate only for minimum conditions of employment,

- to provide adequate procedures to regulate collective bargaining and negotiation,

- to provide for collective agreements and dispute resolution,

- to ensure a negotiating balance between employers and employees, and

- to consult business, labour, and the community representatives whenever changes to labour legislation are considered. This is primarily achieved through the National Economic Development and Labour Council (Nedlac).

National Economic Development and Labour Council

Nedlac is a forum where government meets with organised business, organised labour, and organised community groupings on a national level to discuss and try to reach consensus on issues of social and economic policy. The aim is to make decision making more inclusive and to promote the goals of economic growth and social equity.

Nedlac is funded by the Department of Labour, which is the primary government representative. However other departments such as Trade and Industry, Finance, and Public Works are also involved. Other national departments will be invited to attend when there is an issue that relates to their portfolio.

In this chapter, we are going to focus on employment and provide you with the information required to manage and administer the relationship between you and your employees in the workplace. The most important factor when dealing with employment is to identify and implement the correct wage structures and conditions of employment applicable to your business.

When Jaque sets up her business, she must be aware of what laws govern and protect the employment relationship she has with the people who work for her. She will have to determine whether she falls under a sectoral determination, a bargaining council, or, finally, the BCEA. Once this is clear, she will know what she can lawfully expect of her workers, and what they can lawfully expect of her.

9.3 The Labour Relations Act

The *Labour Relations Act, 66 of 1995* (the LRA), as amended from time to time, is a lengthy and multifaceted piece of legislation. Although it would be wise for you, as a small business owner, to obtain a copy and to keep it on the premises for reference purposes, it is not essential that you read it from cover to cover. You can obtain a copy from your local Department of Labour or labour office or alternatively you can download it from www.labour.gov.za/legislation.

The LRA aims to promote economic development, social justice, harmony, and democracy in the workplace. It sets out to achieve this by providing a framework for regulating the relationship between employees and their unions, on the one hand, and employers and their organisations on the other hand. At the same time, it also encourages employers and employees to regulate relationships between themselves.

The Act provides employees and employers with the right to fair labour practices, to form and join trade unions, to form and join employers' organisations, to organise and bargain collectively, and to engage in strikes and lock-outs. In doing so, it reflects the vision of employees' and employers' rights contained in the Constitution.

The Act also provides for conciliation and negotiation as a way of settling labour disputes. It expects parties to make a genuine attempt to settle disputes through conciliation before going on to the next step, which could be arbitration, adjudication, or industrial action. By providing for a more simplified dispute resolution process, through the Commission for Conciliation, Mediation and Arbitration (CCMA), the Act aims to make available a quick, effective, and inexpensive dispute-resolution mechanism.

As mentioned above, it is not essential that you read and understand the LRA from cover to cover, and for that reason we have chosen not to go into any great detail in the chapter. We have, however, provided a list of the contents, giving you a broad overview of what the Act covers.

Contents of the LRA

Chapter 1: Purpose, application and interpretation

Chapter 2: Freedom of association and general protections

Chapter 3: Collective bargaining

    Part A: Organisational rights

    Part B: Collective agreements

    Part C: Bargaining councils

    Part D: Bargaining councils in the public service

    Part E: Statutory councils

    Part F: General provisions concerning councils

Chapter 4: Strikes and lock-outs

Chapter 5: Workplace forums

Chapter 6: Trade unions and employers' organisations

    Part A: Registration and regulation of trade unions and employers' organisations

9.4 Conditions of employment

As can be seen from the above, the LRA covers many important aspects governing labour relations in South Africa. Equally important, however, are the precise conditions of employment and minimum wages that will apply to your business and to your employees. Finding out and implementing the correct employment conditions from the beginning will save you many a headache in the future.

Minimum conditions of employment for your particular business will be governed by one of the following:

- The *Basic Conditions of Employment Act.* This Act applies to all employers and employees not covered by a Bargaining Council, a Sectoral Determination, or an in-house collective recognition agreement.

- **A Bargaining Council:** This applies to businesses in certain industries located in specific geographical locations where the majority of the employers and the majority of employees come together and agree to negotiate minimum wages and conditions of employment for that sector.

- **A Sectoral (wage) Determination:** This applies to businesses in certain industries located in specific geographical locations where the Department of Labour, after consultation, provides for minimum wages and conditions of employment.

- **A collective (in-house) or recognition agreement:** An 'in-house' recognition agreement comes about as a result of a registered and representative trade union approaching a specific business with a view to negotiating wages and conditions of employment on behalf of the employees. The trade union will be required to prove majority representation of the employees within the specific business and as a result the employers will be required to recognise and negotiate with the trade union.

The best way to establish whether or not your business falls under the *Basic Conditions of Employment Act*, a Bargaining Council, or a Sectoral Determination would be to contact the appropriate industry association, call the Department of Labour or labour office in your immediate area, or alternatively talk to someone already established and running a business in the same industry.

The following section will assist you in establishing which enactment applies to your particular business, and will provide you with a broad understanding of the various conditions of employment that you will be required to implement.

1. Write down what each of the following stands for and explain each of them:

   - LRA,

   - BCEA,

   - Nedlac,

   - CCMA, and

   - Recognition agreement.

2. What does a Bargaining Council do?

3. Who or what governs labour relations in South Africa?

4. Where can you find copies of relevant labour legislation?

5. What labour legislation must you display in your workplace?

9.5 The Basic Conditions of Employment Act

If your business does not fall under a Bargaining Council or a Sectoral Determination, the employment conditions applicable will be provided for under the *Basic Conditions of employment Act* (BCEA)

The BCEA applies to the majority of employers and employees in South Africa and regulates employment conditions such as leave, working hours (ordinary, Sundays, and public holidays), employment contracts, employee records, deductions, pay slips, overtime, and termination.

If you have established that the BCEA applies to your business, you should immediately obtain a copy by contacting your local Department of Labour or labour office. Alternatively, you can download a copy from www.labour.gov.za/legislation. It is a requirement of the BCEA that you display a copy of the Act on your premises. Poster copies can be obtained from the department.

The following sub-sections provide a summary of the most important sections of the *Basic Conditions of Employment Act, 1997*, as amended.

9.5.1 Application

The Act applies to all employees and employers except members of the South African National Defence Force, National Intelligence Agency, South African Secret Service, and unpaid volunteers working for an organisation with a charitable purpose.

The basic conditions of employment contained in the Act form part of the contract of employment of employees covered by the Act. Some, but not all, basic conditions of employment may be varied by individual or collective agreements in accordance with the provisions of the Act.

It is important to note that the Ministerial Determination for Small Business (*Government Gazette*, No. 20587 of 5 November 1999) in terms of the *Basic Conditions of Employment Act* exempts small business, as defined, from a number of provisions contained in the *Basic Conditions of Employment Act* and covers such matters as overtime, the averaging of hours of work, and family responsibility leave.

9.5.2 Regulation of working time

This section covering the regulation of working time does not apply to senior management employees, employees engaged as sales staff who travel, and employees who work less than 24 hours a month.

Ordinary hours of work

No employer shall require or permit an employee to work more than

(a) 45 hours in any week,

(b) nine hours in any day if an employee works for five days or less in a week, or

(c) eight hours in any day if an employee works for more than five days in a week.

Overtime

An employer may not require or permit an employee

(a) to work overtime except by an agreement, or

(b) to work more than ten hours' overtime a week.

> The Small Business Determination permits a business employing fewer than ten employees to increase overtime to a maximum of 15 hours per week for as long as the first ten hours are paid at one and one third times, and the remaining five hours at one and a half times, the employee's wage.

Additional provisions

- An agreement may not require or permit an employee to work more than 12 hours on any day.

- A collective agreement may increase overtime to 15 hours per week for up to two months in any period of 12 months.

- Overtime must be paid at 1.5 times the employee's normal wage or an employee may agree to receive paid time off.

Compressed working week

An employee may agree in writing to work up to 12 hours in a day without receiving overtime pay. However, this agreement may not require or permit an

employee to work

(a) more than 45 ordinary hours in any week,

(b) more than ten hours' overtime in any week, or

(c) more than five days in any week.

Averaging of hours of work

A collective agreement may permit the hours of work to be averaged over a period of up to four months. An employee who is bound by such a collective agreement may not work more than

(a) an average of 45 ordinary hours in a week over the agreed period, or

(b) an average of five hours' overtime in a week over the agreed period.

> The Small Business Determination permits a business employing fewer than ten employees to increase the average overtime (b) above, to ten hours a week over the agreed period.

Meal intervals

An employee must have a meal interval of 60 minutes after five hours' work. However, a written agreement may

(a) reduce the meal interval to 30 minutes, or

(b) dispense with the meal interval for employees who work less than six hours in a day.

Daily and weekly rest period

An employee must have a daily rest period of 12 consecutive hours and a weekly rest period of 36 consecutive hours, which, unless otherwise agreed, must include Sunday.

Pay for work on Sundays

An employee who occasionally works on a Sunday must receive double pay. An employee who ordinarily works on a Sunday must be paid at 1.5 times the normal wage.

However, paid time off in return for working on a Sunday may be agreed upon.

Night work

Employees who work at night between 18h00 and 06h00 must be compensated by payment of an allowance or by a reduction of working hours, and transport must be available. Employees who work regularly after 23:00 and before 06:00 the next day must be informed

(a) of any health and safety hazards, and

(b) of the right to undergo a medical examination.

Public holidays

Employees must be paid their ordinary pay for any public holiday that falls on a working day. Work on a public holiday is by agreement and paid at double the rate, and a public holiday may be exchanged with another day by agreement.

9.5.3 Leave

The section covering leave does not apply to an employee who works less than 24 hours in a month and to leave granted in excess of the leave entitlement under this section.

Annual leave

Employees are entitled to 21 consecutive days' annual leave or by agreement, one day for every 17 days worked or one hour for every 17 hours worked. Leave must be granted not later than six months after the end of the annual leave cycle and an employer must not pay an employee, instead of granting leave, except on termination of employment.

Sick leave

An employee is entitled to six weeks' paid sick leave in a period of 36 months. During the first six months an employee is entitled to one day's paid sick leave for every 26 days worked. An employer may require a medical certificate before paying an employee who is absent for more than two consecutive days or who is frequently absent.

Maternity leave

A pregnant employee is entitled to four consecutive months' maternity leave. A pregnant employee or employee nursing her child is not permitted to perform work that is hazardous to her or her child.

Family responsibility leave

Full-time employees are entitled to three days' paid family responsibility leave per year, on request, when the employee's child is born or sick, or in the event of the death of the employee's spouse or life partner, or the employee's parent, adoptive parent, grandparent, child, adopted child, grandchild, or sibling. An employer may require reasonable proof.

The Small Business Determination permits a business employing fewer than ten employees to conclude a written agreement in terms of which the number of days of annual leave may be reduced by the number of paid days' leave granted on family responsibility leave, at the employee's request.

9.5.4 Particulars of employment and remuneration

This section does not apply to an employee who works less than 24 hours a month for an employer.

Written particulars of employment

An employer must supply an employee, when the employee commences employment, with the following particulars in writing:

- full name and address of the employer,
- name and occupation of the employee, or a brief description of the work,
- various places of work,
- date of employment,
- ordinary hours of work and days of work,
- wage, or the rate and method of calculating wage,
- rate for overtime work,
- any other cash payments,
- any payment in kind and the value thereof,
- frequency of remuneration,
- any deductions,
- leave entitlement,
- period of notice or period of contract,
- description of any council or sectoral determination which covers the employer's business,

- period of employment with a previous employer that counts towards the period of employment, and
- list of any other documents that form part of the contract, indicating a place where a copy of each may be obtained.

Particulars must be revised if the terms of employment change at any time.

Informing employees of their rights

A statement of employees' rights must be displayed at the workplace in official languages used at the workplace.

Keeping of records

Every employer must keep a record containing the following information:

(a) employee's name and occupation,

(b) time worked,

(c) remuneration paid,

(d) date of birth if under 18 years of age, and

(e) any other prescribed information.

Information about remuneration

The following information must be given in writing when the employee is paid:

(a) employer's name and address,

(b) employee's name and occupation,

(c) period of payment,

(d) remuneration in money,

(e) any deduction made from the remuneration,

(f) the actual amount paid, and

(g) if relevant to the calculation of that employee's remuneration,

  (i) employee's rate of remuneration and overtime rate,

  (ii) number of ordinary and overtime hours worked during the period of payment,

  (iii) number of hours worked on a Sunday or public holiday during that period, and

(iv) if an agreement on average working time has been concluded, the total number of ordinary and overtime hours worked in the period of averaging.

Deductions and other acts concerning remuneration

An employer may not deduct money from an employee's remuneration unless

(a) the employee agrees in writing to the deduction of a specific debt, or

(b) the deduction is made in terms of a collective agreement, the law, a court order, or an arbitration award.

A deduction in respect of damage or loss caused by the employee may only be made by agreement and after the employer has followed a fair procedure. Employers must pay deductions and employer contributions to the appropriate benefit funds within seven days.

Calculation of remuneration and wages

Wages are calculated by the number of hours ordinarily worked. The monthly remuneration or wage is four and one-third times the weekly wage. If calculated on a basis other than time, or if the employee's remuneration or wage fluctuates significantly from period to period, any payment must be calculated by reference to remuneration or wage during

(a) the preceding 13 weeks, or

(b) if employed for a shorter period, that period.

Employers and employees should consult a tax schedule published in the *Government Gazette* to determine whether a particular category of payment forms part of an employee's remuneration for the purpose of calculations made in terms of this Act.

9.5.5 Termination of employment

This section does not apply to an employee who works less than 24 hours in a month for an employer.

Notice of termination of employment

A contract of employment may be terminated on notice of not less than

(a) one week, if the employee has been employed for six months or less,

(b) two weeks, if the employee has been employed for more than six months but not more than one year, or

(c) four weeks, if the employee has been employed for one year or more, or if a farm worker or domestic worker has been employed for more than six months.

A collective agreement may shorten the four weeks' notice period to not less than two weeks. Notice must be given in writing except when it is given by an illiterate employee. The notice on termination of employment by an employer in terms of the Act does not prevent the employee challenging the fairness or lawfulness of the dismissal in terms of the *Labour Relations Act, 1995* or any other law.

Severance pay

An employee dismissed for operational requirements or whose contract of employment is terminated in terms of section 38 of the *Insolvency Act, 1936* is entitled to one week's severance pay for every year of service.

Certificate of service

On termination of employment, an employee is entitled to a certificate of service.

Prohibition of employment of children and forced labour

It is a criminal offence to employ a child under 15 years of age. Children under 18 may not be employed to do work inappropriate for their age or that places them at risk. Causing, demanding, or requiring forced labour is a criminal offence.

Variation of basic conditions of employment

A collective agreement concluded by a Bargaining Council may replace or exclude any basic condition of employment except the following:

(a) the duty to arrange working time with regard to the health and safety and family responsibility of employees (S. 7, 9, and 13),

(b) reduce the protection afforded to employees who perform night work (S. 17(3) and(4)),

(c) reduce annual leave to less than two weeks (S. 20),

(d) reduce entitlement to maternity leave (S. 25),

(e) reduce entitlement to sick leave to the extent permitted (S. 22–24), and

(f) prohibition of child and forced labour (S. 48).

Collective agreements and individual agreements may only replace or exclude the basic conditions of employment to the extent permitted by the Act or a sectoral determination (S. 49).

The Minister of Labour may make a determination to vary or exclude a basic condition of employment. This can also be done on application by an employer or employer organisation (S. 50).

A determination may not be granted unless a trade union representing the employees has consented to the variation or has had the opportunity to make representations to the Minister. A copy of any determination must be displayed by the employer at the workplace and must be made available to employees (S. 50).

Sectoral Determinations

Sectoral Determinations may be made to establish basic conditions for employees in a sector and area.

Monitoring, enforcement, and legal proceedings

Labour inspectors must advise employees and employers on their rights and obligations in terms of employment laws. They conduct inspections and investigate complaints, and may question persons and inspect, copy, and remove records and other relevant documents (S. 64 – 66).

An inspector may serve a compliance order on an employer who is not complying with a provision of the Act. The employer may object against the order to the Director-General: Labour, who, after receiving representations, may confirm, modify, or set aside an order. This decision is subject to appeal to the Labour Court (S. 68 – 73).

Employees may not be discriminated against for exercising their rights in terms of the Act (S. 78 – 81).

Presumption as to who is an employee

A person who works for, or provides services to, another person is presumed to be an employee if

(a) his or her manner or hours of work are subject to control or direction,

(b) he or she forms part of the employee's organisation,

(c) he or she has worked for the other person for at least 40 hours per month over the previous three months,

(d) he or she is economically dependent on the other person,

(e) he or she is provided with his or her tools or work equipment, or

(f) he or she only works for, or renders service to, one person.

If one of these factors is present, the person is presumed to be an employee until the employer proves that he or she is not.

General

It is an offence to

(a) obstruct or attempt to influence improperly a person who is performing a function in terms of the Act,

(b) obtain or attempt to obtain any prescribed document by means of fraud, false pretences, or by presenting or submitting a false or forged document,

(c) pretend to be a labour inspector or any other person performing a function in terms of the Act,

(d) refuse or fail to answer fully any lawful question put by a labour inspector or any other person performing a function in terms of the Act,

(e) refuse or fail to comply with any lawful request of, or lawful order by, a labour inspector or any other person performing a function in terms of the Act, and

(f) hinder or obstruct a labour inspector or any other person performing a function in terms of the Act.

Do

1. Read the summary of the BCEA provided above. Identify the terms and conditions that relate to your employees. Ensure that these are included in your conditions of service for your workers.

2. If a labour inspector enters your premises, what is he or she allowed to do? What access must you provide to him or her?

3. What notice period is allowed for termination of employment?

4. Who or what is an employee?

9.6 Bargaining councils

The best way to establish whether or not your business falls under a Bargaining Council would be to contact the appropriate sector or industry association, call the Department of Labour or Labour Office in your immediate area, or alternatively talk to someone running a similar business.

A Bargaining Council is established when a representative group of employers, more often than not one or more employer associations and a representative group of employees, more often than not one or more a trade unions, get together and agree to negotiate minimum wages and conditions of employment for their sector in various demarcated or specified areas.

When this occurs, all industry establishments operating in the same trade and located in the specific area covered by the council are required to join and required to implement the various wage structures and conditions of employment laid down in that particular council or collective agreement.

A collective agreement concluded by a Bargaining Council often has conditions of employment that differ from the *Basic Conditions of Employment Act* for as long as they do not

- lower protection of workers in terms of health and safety and family responsibilities,
- lower annual leave to less than two weeks,
- lower maternity leave in any way,
- lower sick leave in any way,
- lower protection of night workers, or
- allow for any child labour or forced labour.

Examples of Bargaining Councils are provided on the following page (note that this list is not exhaustive).

Industry	Area	Address	Contact
Electrical	National	17 Biccard Street Johannesburg 2001	(011) 339 2312
Laundry, Cleaning & Dyeing	Western Cape	Box 109 Observatory 7935	(021) 448 8000
Furniture Manufacturing	KwaZulu Natal	Box 1554 Durban 4000	(031) 301 7788
Contract Cleaning	KwaZulu Natal	Box 11754 Marine Parade 4056	(031) 309 4880
Fishing Industry	Western Cape	Box 7734 Roggebaai 8012	(021) 421 3369
Laundry, Cleaning & Dyeing	KwaZulu Natal	Box 18414 Umbilo 4001	(031) 307 1860
Furniture Manufacturing	Western Cape	Box 1123 Woodstock 7915	(021) 448 4436
Furniture, Bedding & Upholstery	Gauteng	Box 10467 Johannesburg 2000	(021) 242 9200
Safety & Security	National	Box 1 1269 Centurion 0046	(012) 664 8115
Clothing Industry	National	Box 1142 Woodstock 7915	(021) 460 4000
Metal & Engineering	National	Box 9381 Johannesburg 2000	(011) 838 1075
Motor Industry BC	National	Box 3717 Randburg 2125	(011) 787 9713
Road Freight Industry	National	Private Bag X69 Braamfontein 2017	(011) 403 9990
Building Industry	Free State	Box 693 Bloemfontein 9300	(051) 447 7441
Hairdressing Trade	Western Cape	Box 204 Cape Town 8000	(021) 425 2153
Tearoom, Restaurant & Catering Trades	Pretoria	Box 1256 Pretoria 0001	(012) 322 3493
Entertainment Industry of SA	National	Box 6649 Johannesburg 2000	(011) 403 2167
Building Industry	Western Cape	Private Bag X29 Bellville 7535	(021) 950 7400

9.6.1 Contents of a typical council collective agreement

Although some of the specific employment conditions vary from council to council, in the main, all of the agreements will cover the following conditions:

- **Scope of application:** This section will define the industry, the specific sector, and the magisterial or municipal areas covered by the agreement, and will assist business owners in identifying the correct labour legislation applicable to their particular business.

- **Period of the agreement:** Each agreement, once published, will remain in force for a specified period either until cancelled by the Minister of Labour or until renegotiated by the employer and employee representatives on the council.

- **Special and general provisions:** This is not necessarily included in every council agreement but, if and when provided, usually covers such matters as an extension of the agreement to non-parties or exclusions applicable to certain parties from specified parts of the agreement.

- **Definitions:** A key requirement of all agreements in order to avoid varied interpretations and to ensure a complete understanding and the correct application of the provisions contained therein.

- **Remuneration/wages:** A minimum wage schedule for each sector job category, usually covering a period of two to three years.

- **Payment of remuneration:** This covers the manner in which payment should be made and will include matters concerning casual, fixed term, part–time, and contract employees.

- **Ordinary hours of work, overtime, and payment for overtime:** This section will cover working days, Sundays, ordinary hours of work, spread-overs, meal intervals, overtime, a limitation to overtime, and the payment of overtime and exclusions, if any, from one or more provisions of this section.

- **Paid holidays:** This covers the payment for employees who work or are given time off on a public holiday and how and when the remuneration should be made.

- **Uniforms and protective clothing:** This covers the specific supply, cleaning, replacement, and costs concerning employee uniforms.

- **Prohibition of employment:** This deals with child employment, aliens, and the period before and after confinement for female employees granted maternity leave under the agreement.

- **Contracts of employment:** This will specify the specific details required to be included in an employee's letter or contract of employment and in some cases cover temporary or probation period conditions.

- **Notice of termination of employment:** This gives very specific and detailed requirements concerning the period, the payment, the conditions, and the process of giving notice by either employer to employee or visa versa.
- **Maternity leave:** As a requirement of the *Basic Conditions of Employment Act*, all council agreements will include a comprehensive provision covering the granting, the notice period, and the payment for maternity leave.
- **Annual leave:** Annual leave requirements for the various categories of employees include the manner in which annual leave is requested, granted, and remunerated and will cover the annual closings of a business if applicable.
- **Sick leave:** This covers such aspects as notification, medical certificates, aggregated entitlements, and the payment for sick leave.
- **Meals and transport:** Covers the requirement, the time period, the provision, and the permissible deductions for employee meals, together with the provision of transport during certain periods and for types of employees.
- **Certificate of service:** This requires that employers furnish departing employees with certificates of service under specified conditions.
- **Time/wage and attendance registers:** This covers the register requirements and the recording of both the attendance and time worked by all categories of employees.

In addition to the above, a number, but not all, of the council agreements include provisions covering designated agents, membership, rights, and obligations of both the employer and employee representatives, dispute resolution functions of the council, conciliation functions, exemptions, codes of good practice, freedom of association, expenses of the council, and copies of the required document types.

9.7 Sectoral determinations

The best way to establish whether or not your business would fall under a Sectoral Determination would be to contact the appropriate sector or industry Association. Call the Department of Manpower or Labour Office in your immediate area, or alternatively talk to someone already operating a business in the same industry.

As mentioned earlier, Sectoral Determinations are concluded for specified areas and for specific industries where the majority of the employers and employees have requested the Minister of Labour to regulate minimum wages and conditions of employment.

9.7.1 Current Sectoral Determinations

The following Sectoral Determinations had been published by Department of Labour and were in force at the time of writing:

- **Sectoral Determination 1: Contract Cleaning Sector.** The Contract Cleaning Sectoral Determination regulates wages, working hours, and other basic conditions of employment for contract cleaning workers.

- **Sectoral Determination 2: Civil Engineering Sector.** Special conditions of employment applicable only to employers and employees in the civil engineering sector.

- **Sectoral Determination 5: Learnerships.** A sectoral determination establishing conditions of employment and rates of allowances for learners in South Africa.

- **Sectoral Determination 6: Private Security Sector.** Basic conditions of employment applicable to employers and workers in the private security sector.

- **Sectoral Determination 7: Domestic Workers.** Specific conditions governing the employment of domestic workers.

- **Sectoral Determination 9: Wholesale and Retail Sector.** Basic conditions of employment applicable to employers and workers in the wholesale and retail sector.

- **Sectoral Determination 10: Children in the Performance of Advertising, Artistic and Cultural Activities.** Basic conditions of employment applicable to children in the performing arts and their employers.

- **Sectoral Determination 11: Taxi Sector.** The Taxi Sectoral Determination regulates wages, working hours, and other basic conditions of employment for taxi workers.

- **Sectoral Determination 12: Forestry Sector.** The Forestry Sectoral Determination regulates wages, working hours, and other basic conditions of employment for forestry workers.

- **Sectoral Determination 13: Farm Worker Sector.** Basic conditions of employment for farm workers.

9.7.2 Broad summary of the contents of a Sectoral Determination

Most Sectoral Determinations will include, but are not limited to, the following conditions of employment provisions:

- **Area and scope of the agreement:** It will determine the industry, the type or types of establishment or businesses, and the geographical location of the establishment or business that will be required to adhere to the minimum conditions of employment and the wage schedules contained therein. It is under this section that establishment owners can identify the specific determination that is applicable to their particular establishment.

- **Definitions:** These are a key requirement of all agreements in order to avoid varied interpretations and to ensure a complete understanding and the correct application of the provisions.

- **Remuneration/wages:** Each determination provides a minimum wage schedule, divided into a number of geographical areas, and covering a number of specified job categories for a period of two to three years from the date on which the determination became effective.

- **Payment of remuneration:** This covers the manner in which payment should be made, and will often include matters concerning casual, fixed term, part–time, and contract employees.

- **Ordinary hours of work, overtime, and payment for overtime:** This covers working days, ordinary hours of work, spread-overs, meal intervals, overtime, a limitation to overtime, and the payment of overtime and exclusions, if any, from one or more of the provisions contained within this section.

- **Annual leave:** This covers annual leave requirements for the various categories of employees, including the manner in which annual leave should be requested, granted,and remunerated, and will also include any exclusions, if applicable, from one or more of the provisions contained under this section.

- **Sick leave:** This covers aspects such as notification, medical certificates, aggregated entitlements, the payment for sick leave, and exclusions, if any, from one or more of the provisions contained under this section.

- **Maternity leave:** This deals with the granting, notice period, and payment for maternity leave.

- **Paid holidays and Sundays:** This covers the compensation to full-time employees and casual employees for work on public holidays and Sundays.

- **Ratio:** This provides the ratio of trainees or unqualified employees relative to skilled and qualified employees permitted in the various skill or job categories.

- **Prohibition of employment:** This covers the limitations in terms of the employment of children and in terms of the employment of pregnant employees before and after confinement.

- **Uniforms and special clothing:** This provides for the issue, cleaning, and maintenance of employee uniforms and any costs associated therewith.

- **Termination of contract of employment:** This deals with the period of notice, the payment, the employers' obligations, and the employee rights required in terms of any desire on behalf of the employer to terminate the service of an employee.

- **Certificate of service:** This deals with the issue of a certificate of service to an employee, the required contents to be included, and other matters concerning the certificate upon any termination of any contract of employment.

- **Attendance register:** This provides for the recording, in the specified format, of all particulars relating to every employee in terms of the days of the week and hours of the day worked by that employee.

9.8 Codes of good practice

Nedlac and the Department of Labour have published Codes of Good Practice that will help you in regulating the employment relationship with your employees. Although you are not required by law to implement the codes, they are extremely helpful and it is recommended that you obtain copies of the codes relevant to your business. You can either obtain copies from your local Department of Manpower or Labour Office or you can download them from the Department of Labour's website at www.labour.gov.za. These Codes of Good practice are listed below

- **Arrangement of Working Time:** Information and guidelines on shift work and night work and their impact on workers' health and safety.

- **Disability in the Workplace:** The code is a guide for employers and workers on key aspects of promoting equal opportunities and fair treatment for people with disabilities.

- **Employment Equity Plans:** The objective of this code is to provide guidelines of good practice in terms of the requirements of the *Employment Equity Act.*

- **Handling Sexual Harassment Cases:** This code aims to assist in the elimination of sexual harassment in the workplace. It provides procedures to deal with the problem and prevent it from recurring.

- **Integration of Employment Equity into Human Resources Policies:** This code identifies areas of human resources that are key to employment equity, which can be used to advance equity objectives.

- **Key Aspects of HIV/Aids and Employment:** The code's objective is to provide guidelines for employers, workers, and trade unions on how to manage HIV/Aids within the workplace.

- **Key Aspects on the Employment of People with Disabilities:** A guide for employers and workers on promoting equal opportunities and fair treatment for people with disabilities.

- **National Code of Practice for the Evaluation of Training Providers for Lifting Machine Operators:** This Code of Good Practice is to provide clarity and direction to all stakeholders directly or indirectly related to the accreditation and provision of training to lifting machine and equipment operators.

- **Pregnancy:** Provides for the protection of workers during pregnancy and after the birth of a child.

---

1. How would a Bargaining Council collective agreement apply to your business?

2. How would a Sectoral Determination apply to your business?

3. How would you find out if you fall under a Bargaining Council or a Sectoral Determination?

4. How would Codes of Good Practice apply to your business? Where would you be able to source and access applicable codes?

9.9 Examples and templates

Please note that the following annexures have been provided as a guide only. As an employer you will be required to add specific information relevant to your particular business and will also need to ensure that you comply with any other statutory requirement concerning each annexure. For example, a Bargaining Council agreement may require you to add additional information or complete a specific form relevant to that particular council.

9.9.1 Example 1: Payslip

The *Basic Conditions of Employment Act* requires employers to give their workers a pay slip. Employers must give the pay slip to employees at the workplace or a place agreed to by the employees and this must occur during the employees' normal working hours.

Letterhead: Name of business and logo
Address

Employee No: _____   Date engaged: _____

Employee name: _____   ID Number: _____

Address: _____   Tax ref number: _____

Position: _____

Payment method: _____   Pay date: _____

Bank: _____   Payslip number: _____

Branch: _____

Account number: _____

Supplementary Info	Earnings	Deductions
Earnings to date: R.....	Basic salary: R.....	Tax: R......
		UIF: R......
		Medical aid: R ......
Tax to date: R......		
Total employer contributions: R		
	Gross pay: R	Total deductions: R ......
UIF: R......		
Medical aid: R......		
Leave days:		Net Pay: R ....

9.9.2 Example 2: Contract of employment

**Contract of Employment
entered into between:**

....

(herein after referred to as 'the employer')
Address of employer:

....

....

....

....

and

....

(herein after referred to as 'the employee')

1. Commencement

This contract will begin on .... and continue until terminated as set out in clause 4.

2. Place of work

....

3. Job description

Job title ....

[e.g. Sales person, chef, shop assistant etc]

Duties ....

....

....

....

4. Termination of employment

Either party can terminate this agreement with four weeks' written notice. In the case where an employee is illiterate, notice may be given by that employee verbally.

5. Wage

5.1	The employee's wage shall be paid in cash on the last working day of every week/month and shall be:	R............
5.2	The employee shall be entitled to the following allowances/payment in kind:	
5.2.1	A weekly/monthly transport allowance of	R............
5.2.2	Meals per week/month to the value of	R............
5.2.3	Accommodation per week/month to the value of	R............
5.3	The total value of the above remuneration shall be	R............
	[The total of clauses 5.1 to 5.2.3] [Modify or delete clauses 5.2.1 to 5.2.3 as needed]	

5.4 The employer shall review the employee's salary/wage once a year.

6. Hours of work

6.1 Normal working hours will be from ………… a.m. to …………. p.m. on Mondays to Fridays and from ……………a.m. to ………..p.m. on Saturdays.

6.2 Overtime will only be worked if agreed upon between the parties from time to time.

6.3 The employee will be paid for overtime at the rate of one and a half times his/her total wage as set out in clause 5.3.

7. Meal intervals

The employee agrees to a lunch break of one hour/30 minutes (delete which is not applicable). Lunchtime will be taken from ………… to …………… daily.

8. Sunday work

Any work on Sundays will be by agreement between the parties from time to time.
If the employee works on a Sunday he/she shall be paid double the wage for each hour worked.

9. Public holidays

The employee will be entitled to all official public holidays on full pay.
If an employee does not work on a public holiday, he/she shall receive normal payment for that day.
If the employee works on a public holiday he/she shall be paid double.

10. Annual leave

10.1 The employee is entitled to……….. days' paid leave after every 12 months of continuous service. Such leave is to be taken at times convenient to the employer and the employer may require the employee to take his/her leave at such times as coincide with those of the employer.

11. Sick leave

11.1 During every sick leave cycle of 36 months the employee will be entitled to an amount of paid sick leave equal to the number of days the employee would normally work during a period of six weeks.

11.2 During the first six months of employment the employee will be entitled to one day's paid sick leave for every 26 days worked.

11.3 The employee is to notify the employer as soon as possible in case of his/her absence from work through illness.

12. Maternity leave

(Tick the applicable clauses in the space provided).

12.1	The employee will be entitled to …………. days' maternity leave without pay; or	
12.2	The employee will be entitled to ………… days' maternity leave on ………… pay	

13. Family responsibility leave

The employee will be entitled to three days' family responsibility leave during each leave cycle.

14. Deductions from remuneration

The employer may not deduct any monies from the employee's wage unless the employee has agreed to this in writing on each occasion.

15. Accommodation

(Tick the applicable boxes).

15.1	The employee will be provided with accommodation for as long as the employee is in the service of the employer, and which shall form part of his/her remuneration package	
15.2	The accommodation may only be occupied by the worker, unless prior arrangement with the employer.	
15.3	Prior permission should be obtained for visitors who wish to stay the night. However where members of the employees direct family are visiting, such permission will not be necessary.	

16. Clothing (Delete this clause if not applicable)

………… sets of uniforms will be supplied to the employee by the employer and will remain the property of the employer.

17. Other conditions of employment or benefits

..............................☐
..............................☐
..............................☐
..............................☐
..............................☐
..............................☐
..............................☐

18. General

Any changes to this agreement will only be valid if they are in writing and have been agreed and signed by both parties.

THUS DONE AND SIGNED AT ………………….. ON THIS ………… DAY OF
…………………………. 20...

……………………………………………   ……………………………………………………
EMPLOYER   EMPLOYEE

Witnesses:
………………………………………………………………
………………………………………………………………

9.9.3 Example 3: Wage register

The *Basic Conditions of Employment Act* requires that employers keep records of time worked and pay received by workers. This form provides a template for employee records showing time worked and pay received. Employers must keep this form for three years after the last entry. Employers who keep this record do not have to keep any other records of working time and pay of their workers. Workers have the right to inspect the records.

BCEA 2

WAGE REGISTER

NAME OF EMPLOYEE: ....□

IDENTITY NO□

PAY PERIOD: .... BASIC WAGE: .... OCCUPATION: ....

MANNER OF PAYMENT   □ PER HOUR   □ PER DAY   □ PER WEEK

□ PER FORTNIGHT   □ PER MONTH

CALCULATION OF WAGES		
Ordinary hours worked	Amount due	R
Overtime worked	Amount due	R
Hours worked on Sundays	Amount due	R
Hours worked on Public holidays ..	Amount due	R
Allowances: Shift		
Housing		
Transport		
Medical		
Other: (specify)		
....		
Total		**R**
Total		**R**
Authorised deductions: P.A.Y.E.		
UIF		
Union		
Medical		
Retirement		
Other (Full details)		
....		
Total		**R**
TOTAL AMOUNT DUE		**R**

SIGNATURE OF EMPLOYEE

DATE

9.9.4 Example 4: Attendance register

The *Basic Conditions of Employment Act* requires employers to keep record of the attendance of their workers. The form can be completed by either the employer or the employee. Employers must keep this form for three years after the last entry. If employers keep this record, they do not have to keep any other records of their workers' attendance.

BCEA 3

BASIC CONDITIONS OF EMPLOYMENT ACT, 1997
ATTENDANCE REGISTER

Note – Employees must make entries only in the section of the register reserved for their use

Name of employee ....

Employee number ....

Entries to be made by employees or if the employee is unable, the employer

Date	Day of week	Signature	Starting time	Meal Intervals		Finishing time	Total number of hours worked		Overtime worked			Public holidays worked			Remarks
				Off	On		Each day	Each week	From	To	Total hours worked	From	To	Total hours worked	

Year: ....
Month: ....

9.9.5 Example 5: Certificate of service

The *Basic Conditions of Employment Act* requires employers to give their workers a Certificate of Service when their employment is ended. This will serve as proof that the employee worked for the employer. Employers must give this form to workers when they end their employment. The reason for ending the employment must only be completed if workers ask for it.

BCEA 5

BASIC CONDITIONS OF EMPLOYMENT ACT, 1997
Section 42
READ THIS FIRST

CERTIFICATE OF SERVICE

I ....
(name and designation of person)

of

....
(full name of employer)

WHAT IS THE PURPOSE OF THIS FORM?
This form is proof of employment with a employer.

address: ....

....

WHO FILLS IN THIS FORM?
The employer.

in the .... (trade)

declare that

WHERE DOES THIS FORM GO?
To the employee.

....
(full name of employer)

....
(I.D. no.)

INSTRUCTIONS
This form may be issued upon termination of employment.

was in employment

from .... until ....

NOTE
In terms of section 42(g) the reason for termination of employment must only be given if requested by the employee.

as

....
(type of work/occupation)

....

This is only a model and not a prescribed form.
Completing a document in another format containing the same information is sufficient compliance with the regulation.

any other information ....

On termination of service this employee was earning: R ....

.... (amount in words)

per hour   per day   per week   per fortnight   per month   per year

....
Employer's signature   Date

9.10 Self-evaluation

1. List the forms that you will need to manage your staff in accordance with labour legislation.

2. Check that you already have these documents on file, or develop them if you still need them.

10 Health and safety
in the workplace

10.1 Learning outcomes

After you have studied this chapter you should be able to

- explain the framework of safety legislation for the workplace,

- know your responsibilities as an employer,

- record and report on accidents in the workplace,

- ensure compliance with general safety legislation and industry-specific regulations, and

- determine the extent to which human rights are recognised in your business, with relation to the Constitution and HIV/Aids.

10.2 Introduction

Every year, thousands of working hours are lost due to accidents that occur in the workplace. This leads to a reduction in productivity for the country in general and for business in particular. Sometimes, in the case of serious injury, disablement or death can occur, which is a very high price to pay for not ensuring that safe work practices are enforced.

Occupational health and safety legislation aims at making the workplace as safe and healthy as possible for employees. If you apply and maintain the requirements of this legislation, the risk of accidents in the workplace is reduced and the demand on the compensation fund is reduced.

Workplace accidents can happen very easily, especially in the manufacturing, agricultural, and hospitality industries. Hazardous work, flammable liquids, electricity, gas, chemicals, machinery, and dangerous implements are all found in many work environments. It is up to you as the business owner to protect your business, yourself, and equally importantly your workers against any accident, injury, or occupational disease.

Hazardous describes a substance or action that is dangerous or may cause injuries, disease, or death.

In our example of Jaque's Treats, Jaque will have to be very conscious about safety at her premises. Her staff will be working with knives, heat, steam, stoves, glass, and so on. Furthermore, they will be working with chemicals for cleaning, and will have to wear some form of safety clothing or equipment such as overalls, gloves, and caps. She will have to be very aware of safety in order to look after her staff properly. She must have a good understanding of what is expected of her as an employer, and must tell her staff about what is expected of them as employees.

Jaque will also have to keep safety equipment in her kitchen, as well as a first-aid box in case of accidents. In the event of an accident, she must know how to deal with it on the spot, and how to report it to the authorities later. She will also have to help her staff claim for compensation for any injuries suffered in the workplace. Safety is a very serious responsibility that she must fully understand to ensure that both her workers and her business are protected.

This chapter should be read in conjunction with sections 6.10 and 6.11 in chapter 6 on building regulations for premises, as they relate to infrastructural requirements, provision of fire and safety equipment, and so forth.

10.3 Sources of occupational health and safety legislation

It is all but impossible to regulate safety at work comprehensively through an Act of Parliament. If you think of the diverse safety requirements for all the different industries operating in South Africa, you will realise that no single piece of legislation can provide generic health and safety standards. Each industry has its own particular production processes with specific machinery and operating equipment unique to its requirements.

The Department of Labour has developed a framework of legislation that serves to protect employers and employees from accidents and injuries in the workplace. *The Occupational Health and Safety Act, 85 of 1993* (OHS) determines the responsibilities of the employer and the employee and makes provision for the establishment and operation of safety committees and representatives.

In terms of this Act, all regulations provided for under the original *Machinery and Occupational Safety Act, 6 of 1983* (MOS) remain in force and effect. The OHS and the regulations made in terms of the MOS therefore interface and cover different aspects of safety.

A range of laws, regulations, and codes of practice govern workplace health and safety. The following diagram depicts the occupational health and safety regulatory framework.

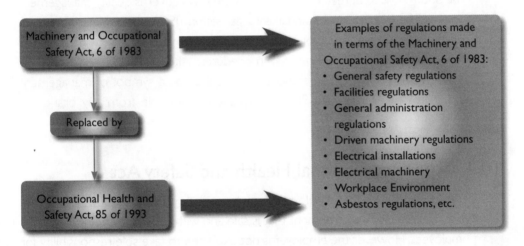

Figure 10.1 Occupational health and safety regulatory framework

As can be seen in figure 10.1, the OHS replaced the MOS in 1993, but the regulations contained in the MOS remain in effect. Details of this legislation will be discussed later in this chapter.

10.3.1 National Occupational Safety Association

The National Occupational Safety Association (NOSA) is an organisation that assists businesses to identify and control safety issues in the workplace. It has a safety system that provides a structure for applying the relevant safety laws needed in each organisation. Any branch of NOSA may be contacted for further information regarding safety systems and training.

10.3.2 South African Bureau of Standards

The South African Bureau of Standards (SABS) also governs quality-management systems. The International Standards Organisation (ISO) has a range of systems for the quality assurance of various sectors of industry, which includes the development of safe operational procedures. Although it is voluntary, the ISO series is becoming internationally recognised as a symbol of management and safety excellence. ISO 9000 information is available from any branch of SABS.

10.4   The Occupational Health and Safety Act

The OHS requires that employers implement and maintain, as far as reasonably practicable, a work environment that is safe and without risk to the health of the employees. However, the employer is not expected to take sole responsibility for health and safety.

The Act is based on the principle that dangers in the workplace must be addressed by communication and cooperation between both the employees and the employers. They are required to share the responsibility for health and safety in the workplace. Both parties must pro-actively identify dangers and develop control measures to make the workplace safe. As a result, the employer and the workers are involved in a process in which health and safety representatives inspect the workplace regularly and report back to a health and safety committee. The committee will, when required, submit reports and recommendations to senior management.

> The purpose of the OHS is to provide for the health and safety of persons at work or in connection with the use of plant and machinery. It also provides for the protection of persons other than persons at work from hazards arising from or in connection with the activities of persons at work.

The Minister of Labour may, in terms of the Act, issue various health and safety regulations and standards covering specific processes and activities. These regulations, as well as the General Safety Regulations previously mentioned, have to be read together with the Act.

The Act applies to all workers except those employed in the mining sector and certain employees in the aviation sector.

10.4.1 Occupational Health and Safety Council

The Act makes provision for the establishment of the Occupational Health and Safety Council whose responsibility it is to set up workplace policies. They are also responsible for ensuring that any hazardous or potentially harmful situations are investigated quickly and that the necessary steps are taken to address the matter.

Guidelines, policies, standards, and regulatory changes and/or additions will be established and reviewed on an ongoing basis by the council. Notice will be given to employees and employers of changes and action(s) required to minimise the chance of accidents and incidents by adequately addressing unsafe or hazardous conditions and/or substances.

10.4.2 Enforcement and inspections

The Chief Directorate of Occupational Health and Safety of the Department of Labour is the authority that administers the OHS. Provincial offices have been established and inspectors have been appointed to carry out inspections and investigations.

There are two kinds of inspection: planned and unplanned. Inspections are usually planned on the basis of accident statistics, the presence of hazardous substances, such as the use of benzene in laundries, or the use of dangerous machinery in the workplace. Unplanned inspections, on the other hand, usually arise from requests or complaints by workers, employers, or members of the public. These complaints or requests are treated confidentially.

10.4.3 Powers of inspectors

In order to fulfil their duties, inspectors have fairly far-reaching and broad powers. Inspectors may

- enter a workplace or premises where machinery or hazardous substances are being used, at any reasonable time, and without notice,

- request or serve a summons on persons to appear before them,

- request that any documents be submitted to them,

- investigate and make copies of such documents,

- demand an explanation about any entries recorded in such documents,

- inspect any condition or article and take samples of it,

- seize any article that may be used as evidence,

- barricade, fence, or restrict access to any area where danger exists, and

- investigate any serious incidents and report, if necessary, the outcome to the Director of Public Prosecutions.

The processes of investigations, formal enquiries, and appeals regarding incidents resulting in injury, illness, or death of an employee are set out. Employers and workers must comply with the directions, subpoenas, requests, or orders of inspectors.

10.4.4 Duties of employers towards workers

The OHS places the main responsibility to bring about and maintain a safe and healthy work environment *on the employer*. Responsibility for the implementation of the Act is on the chief executive officer (CEO) or the most senior person in charge of the company.

The employer must therefore ensure that the workplace is free from hazardous substances, articles, equipment, and processes that may cause injury, damage, or disease. Where this is not possible, the employer must inform workers of the dangers, how they may be prevented, and how to work safely, and the employer must provide other protective measures for a safe workplace.

The Act makes provision for many additional aspects of health and safety in the workplace to which employers must comply. These include, but are not limited to,

- duties aimed at ensuring a safe and healthy workplace,
- duty to inform, and
- reporting duties.

1. Advise Jaque on her responsibilities to her staff under the OHS Act.

2. How can you as an employer advise your staff about their responsibilities about safety in their workplace?

3. Draw a safety poster that is applicable in your own premises.

4. How and where will you find out if there are specific safety regulations governing your type of business?

5. What are the consequences or penalties for not conforming to safety requirements or legislation?

6. Determine whether you need any safety committees, forums, or representatives in your business. If not, how will you ensure that safety is prioritised and inspections and safe working practices carried out?

10.4.5 Employees' rights and duties

Although the Act places primary responsibility for health and safety in the workplace on the employer, the employer is not expected to take sole responsibility. The Act is based on the principle that dangers in the workplace must be addressed by both the employer and employees. Therefore, employees also have certain duties which are specifically covered in the Act.

It is the duty of the worker to

- know his or her rights and duties as contained in the OHS Act,
- cooperate with the employer,
- give information to an inspector from the Department of Labour if he or she should require it,
- carry out any lawful instruction which the employer or authorised person prescribes with regard to health and safety,
- comply with the rules and procedures that the employer gives him or her,
- wear the prescribed safety clothing or use the prescribed safety equipment where it is required,
- report unsafe or unhealthy conditions to the employer or health and safety representative as soon as possible,

- report an accident that he or she is involved in that may influence his or her health or cause injury, to the employer and authorised person or the health and safety representative as soon as possible, but no later than by the end of the shift, and

- take care of his or her own health and safety, as well as that of other persons who may be affected by his or her actions or negligence to act. This includes playing at work. Many people have been injured and even killed owing to horseplay in the workplace, which is considered a serious contravention.

Employees must observe the following:

- inform the employer of a hazard,
- report any incident within the same shift,
- carry out instruction in accordance with the Act,
- cooperate with the employer in complying with the Act, and
- not act in such a way as to place themselves or others at risk

An employee has a duty not to interfere with or misuse any object that has been provided in the interest of health and safety. A person may, for example, not remove a safety guard from a machine and use the machine or allow anybody else to use it without such a guard.

10.5 Health and safety representatives

The OHS Act provides for the appointment of health and safety representatives and health and safety committees in the workplace.

Every employer who has more than 20 employees in his or her employment at any workplace must appoint in writing health and safety representatives for that workplace.

Health and safety representatives are full-time employees nominated or elected after consultation and agreement is reached between the employers and employees. They should also be familiar with the circumstances and conditions prevailing in the specific area of the workplace for which they are designated. Agreement must be reached on the period of office and specific functions of the health and safety representatives.

> **D**   **Designated** means specified or identified.

A representative must be designated for every workplace consisting of 20 or more workers. Therefore, where only 19 workers are employed, it is not necessary to designate a representative. However, the rest of the Act still applies.

In the case of shops and offices, one representative must be designated for every 100 workers or part thereof. For example, one representative must be designated in the case of 21 to 100 workers. But two representatives must be designated where 101 to 200 workers are employed, and so forth.

In the case of other workplaces, one representative must be designated for every 50 workers or part thereof. For example, one representative must be designated in the case of 21 to 50 workers. But two representatives must be designated where 51 to 100 workers are employed.

> Determine where your business fits in relation to the requirements listed above. Do you have to designate a safety representative in your business? This is particularly important in small factories or processing plants where machinery is used, or other industries such as construction where safety is also very important.

10.5.1 Functions and duties of health and safety representatives

All activities regarding the designation, function, and training of representatives must be performed during normal working hours. Health and safety representatives are entitled to do the following:

- **Health and safety audits:** Representatives may check the effectiveness of health and safety measures by means of health and safety audits.
- **Identify potential dangers:** Representatives may identify potential dangers in the workplace and report them to the health and safety committee or the employer.
- **Investigate incidents:** Collaborate with the employer to investigate incidents, and also investigate complaints from workers regarding health and safety matters, and report about them in writing.

- **Make representations:** Representatives may make representations regarding the safety of the workplace to the employer or the health and safety committee or, where the representations are unsuccessful, to an inspector.

- **Inspections:** As far as inspections are concerned, representatives may

  ○ inspect the workplace after notifying the employer of the inspection,

  ○ participate in discussions with inspectors at the workplace and accompany inspectors on inspections,

  ○ inspect documents, and

  ○ with the consent of their employer, be accompanied by a technical advisor during an inspection.

- **Attend committee meetings:** Representatives may attend health and safety committee meetings.

10.6   Health and safety committees

The OHS Act also makes provision for the establishment and duties of health and safety committees. These committees consist of the health and safety representatives, and any other employees as deemed necessary for the effective execution of their duties. Such other members may include the CEO (who has ultimate safety responsibility), or maintenance staff who will assist in attending to safety hazards.

Health and safety committees are formed to initiate, promote, maintain, and review measures of ensuring the health and safety of workers. *They should be established when there are two or more health and safety representatives in a workplace.* The employer determines the number of committee members, based on the following:

- If only one committee has been established for a workplace, all the representatives must be members of that committee.

- If two or more committees have been established for a workplace, each representative must be a member of at least one of those committees.

Therefore, every representative must be a member of a committee. The employer may also nominate other persons to represent him or her on a committee, but such nominees may not be more than the number of representatives designated on that committee.

Committees are entitled to meet whenever it is necessary, but at least once every three months. The committee determines the time and place. The procedures adopted at a meeting are determined by the members of the committee, who elect the chairperson and determine his or her period of office, meeting procedures, and so on.

The Act also covers all of the various responsibilities and functions of the health and safety committees, and in addition makes provision for enforcement, prosecution, and penalties.

Below is a health and safety compliance table, which outlines who is responsible, what actions they are responsible for, and when these actions are to be taken.

Who	What	When
Department of Labour	Enforcement and inspection	Continuous, planned, and unplanned

Employers	• Duty to inform
	 • Reporting duties
	 • Operational duties:
	   - Identify potential hazards
	   - Establish precautionary measures to protect workers
	   - Provide information, instructions, training, and supervision
	   - Not permit anyone to carry on with any task unless the necessary precautionary measures have been taken
	   - Comply with the Act
	   - Enforce control measures
	   - Ensure establishment of health and safety committees
	   - Overall responsibility for health and safety
		Continuous

Employees	• Know rights and duties • Take care of own health and safety • Cooperate with the employer • Give information to an inspector from the Department of Labour if needed • Carry out instructions with regard to health and safety • Comply with safety rules and procedures • Wear the prescribed safety clothing or use the prescribed safety equipment where it is required • Report unsafe or unhealthy conditions • Report incidents	Continuous
Health and safety representatives	• Review health and safety measures • Identify potential hazards • Assist in examining the cause of any accident	Continuous Regularly

Who	What	When
	• Investigate any/all complaints by employees in relation to health and safety at work • Make representation on any matters arising from the above • Inspect the premises • Participate in consultations with inspectors and accompany inspectors on inspections • Attend meetings of the health and safety committee	
Health and safety committees	• Make recommendations to the employer or to an inspector regarding any matter affecting health or safety • Discuss any incident at the workplace in which or in consequence of which any person was injured, became ill, or died, • Perform any other functions as may be prescribed • Keep records of any recommendations made to the employer, or any report made to an inspector	Meet a minimum of once every three months

10.7   Safety regulations under the OHS Act

Depending on the type of business that you are operating, you will have to conform to various safety regulations. There are a number of them, applying to different industries, and they can be downloaded from the Department of Labour's website at www.labour.gov.za under the 'Occupational Health and Safety Programme' icon.

The General Safety Regulations 1031 will apply to most industries and will govern the safety of workers in the workplace and the safety standards and guidelines for the workplace under the following headings:

- personal safety equipment and facilities (goggles, helmets, visors, gloves, and so on),

- intoxication in the workplace,

- notices and signs for the workplace,

- first aid, emergency equipment, and procedures,

- use and storage of flammable liquids,

- work in confined spaces,

- work in elevated positions,

- work in danger of engulfment,

- stacking of articles,
- welding, flame cutting, soldering, and similar operations,
- operating trains,
- suspension of building work,
- roof work,
- demolition and excavation,
- ladders,
- ramps, and
- scaffolding frameworks and platforms

If your business includes any of the operations mentioned above, it will be a good idea to get these regulations to ensure that you meet these safety standards in order to protect yourself, your business, and your workers.

There are many other regulations and notices promulgated by the Department of Labour that may be applicable to your business. The list of these, which can all be downloaded from the Department of Labour's website, is as follows:

Safety Regulations under the OHS Act

- **OHS - Asbestos Regulations 2001:** Applies to every person who carries out work at a workplace that may expose them to asbestos dust.

- **OHS - Certificate of Competency:** Occupational Health and Safety regulation that provides the parameters for applying for and obtaining a Certificate of Competency for mechanical engineering.

- **OHS - Construction Regulations 2003:** Occupational Health and Safety regulation regarding all construction activities.

- **OHS - Diving Regulations:** Occupational Health and Safety regulation regarding all diving activities.

- **OHS - Driven Machinery Regulations:** Occupational Health and Safety regulation regarding all aspects concerning driven machinery at the workplace.

- **OHS - Electrical Installation Regulations:** Occupational Health and Safety regulation regarding electrical installations and providing guidelines for all users and employers concerned.

- **OHS - Electrical Machinery Regulations:** Occupational Health and Safety regulation regarding electrical machinery.

- **OHS - Environmental Regulation for Workplaces:** Occupational Health and Safety regulation of parameters for a secure working environment.

- **OHS - Explosives Regulation:** Occupational Health and Safety regulation regarding explosives.

- **OHS - Facilities Regulations:** Occupational Health and Safety regulations regarding facilities that must be provided by employers at the workplace for workers, to improve working conditions for all.

- **OHS - General Administrative Regulations:** The General Administrative Regulations provide the administrative procedure of the Occupational Health and Safety Act.

- **OHS - General Safety Regulations:** Occupational health and safety regulation regarding the general safety of workers at the workplace.

- **OHS - Hazardous Biological Agents:** Occupational Health and safety regulation regarding all aspects of working with hazardous biological agents.

- **OHS - Hazardous Chemical Substances:** Occupational Health and Safety regulation on all aspects of working with hazardous chemical substances.

- **OHS - Lift, Escalator and Passenger Conveyor Regulations:** Occupational Health and Safety regulation providing guidelines for lifts, escalators and passenger conveyors.

- **OHS - Major Hazard Installation:** Occupational Health and safety regulation regarding major hazard installation.

- **OHS - Noise-induced Hearing Loss:** Occupational Health and Safety regulation concerning noise-induced hearing loss at the workplace.

- **OHS - Vessels under Pressure Regulations:** Occupational Health and Safety regulation regarding boilers and vessels under pressure.

There are also a number of other additional documents on the website that you may need, depending on the type of business that you are running.

Vusi and Abel have a small printing works employing 25 people:

- What safety legislation will apply to their business?

- Where will they find copies of this legislation?

- Who will be able to assist them in ensuring that they are complying with the legislation?

- What would the consequences be if they do not comply with safety legislation?

10.8   Compensation for Occupational Injuries and Diseases Act

The Workmen's Compensation Act was replaced by the *Compensation for Occupational Injuries and Diseases Act, 100 of 1993* (COIDA). The objective of the Act is to provide compensation for disablement caused by injuries and diseases sustained as a result of the work and/or working conditions under which the person is placed. The COIDA applies to accidents arising from and in the course of an employee's employment.

All employees, regardless of their earnings, are covered under this Act. The Act provides for loss of earnings but not for pain and suffering incurred. All full-time and casual employees are covered by the Act, with the exceptions of

- members of the SA National Defence Force,

- members of the SA Police Services, and

- domestic workers.

The COIDA defines an employee as any person who has entered into (or works under) a contract of service, a contract of apprenticeship, or a contract of learnership with an employer, whether the contract is express or implied, oral or in writing, and whether the remuneration is calculated by time or by work done, or in cash or kind.

10.8.1 Registration for the payment of compensation

Any employer who employs one or more employees at his or her business is required to register with the Compensation Commissioner in Pretoria in terms of the COIDA. The process is explained in chapter 7.

Records must be kept of employees' wages paid and time worked, and a statement must be submitted to the Compensation Commissioner before the end of March each year. Based on the information supplied to the Commissioner, an amount is determined, which is to be paid to the Compensation Fund within 30 days of a date specified by the Commissioner. These amounts cannot be recovered from the employees.

10.8.2 Reporting of accidents and occupational diseases

The General Safety Regulations and Section 24 of the *Occupational Health and Safety Act* stipulate that injuries and accidents must be reported. The injuries and accidents to be reported are those of a serious nature in which professional medical attention is needed, and from which absence from work will occur.

Employees must notify the manager of an accident on the same day. The accident report form must be completed immediately and a copy sent with the person to the doctor. On the next page is an example of an accident report form.

When the accident report form has been completed, organisational procedures regarding medical reports and claims forms should be completed by the responsible person. All incidents and injuries requiring formal attention or on-site first aid should be recorded in an accident book, usually kept by the supervisor or manager. This is to ensure that any recurring problems are dealt with and prevented from happening again. They also serve as a record of incidents, should formal inquiries be held after an incident occurred.

The report of the accident is followed by the following documents:

- first medical report,
- progress/final medical report, and
- resumption (this must be completed and submitted before payment will be made).

Accident report form			
Details of person injured:			
Surname	First names	Age	Date of birth
Department:		Position:	
Date of accident:	Time:	Was the accident recorded in the accident book?	
How did the accident occur?			
Nature of injuries:			
Was first aid given?		By whom:	
Was the injured person sent to a doctor, medical centre or hospital? (Give details)If so, accompanied by whom?			
Name(s) of witness(es) of the accident:			
Any previous accident that may have been due to the same cause:			
Was the accident caused or contributed to by any defect in working conditions or premises, or the conditions of the equipment or utensils used?			
Signature of person reporting the accident:			
Date:			

The Compensation Commissioner must be contacted within seven days of the accident. This can be done by phoning your local office of the Department of Labour.

A claim for compensation in terms of the COIDA must be lodged within 12 months of the date of the accident. Employers are advised to make inquiries at the offices of the Compensation Commissioner regarding the procedures to follow when reporting an occupational injury. Workmen's compensation claims may be made on forms WCL 1 and 2, which may be obtained from any Department of Labour who will provide instruction on all further procedures and documentation in the event of a compensation claim.

Failing or delaying to report an accident or alleged accident is a criminal offence. The Commissioner may also impose a penalty on the employer, which could be the full amount of the claim. The employer is liable for the payment of compensation for the first three months from the date of the occupational injury, and will be refunded by the Commissioner.

> **D**   A **penalty** is a punishment for an offence.

Copies of COIDA and relevant forms are available from any office of the Department of Labour.

10.9   HIV/Aids in the workplace

The management of HIV/Aids in the workplace has become a particularly important factor in the ongoing health and well-being of employees. Many employers and employees do not know that the Constitution includes various rights for people living with HIV/Aids. As a result, both employers and employees may unwittingly do things that are in fact illegal and can have serious consequences.

10.9.1 Human rights and laws regarding the handling of HIV/Aids issues in the workplace

Notwithstanding their constitutional rights, many people living with or affected by HIV/Aids are discriminated against and stigmatised in the workplace. Currently, there are a number of Acts of Parliament that govern the workplace environment. Of these, however, there are two in particular that deal with HIV/Aids:

1. The **Labour Relations Act** makes it illegal to dismiss anyone for illness ('incapacity') without doing the following:

    - finding out whether that employee is indeed permanently unable to work, and
    - making every effort to try to place that employee in a job that he or she can cope with.

2. The **Employment Equity Act** makes it illegal for an employer
   - to force an employee or prospective employee to have an HIV test without first getting permission from the Labour Court (only under very specific circumstances will the Labour Court give such permission), or
   - to refuse to employ an HIV-positive person or dismiss an employee because of his or her HIV status.

Other important facts

- An employee with HIV is not required to reveal his or her HIV status to the employer. However, if an HIV-positive employee does disclose his or her status, he or she may benefit if management is understanding and provides some form of help, treatment, and support.

- If an employer or co-worker becomes aware of an employee's HIV status, they are expected to keep such information confidential, unless the employee with HIV gives specific consent for the information to be disclosed.

- No employee may refuse to work with a fellow employee with HIV. Such refusal should lead to disciplinary action.

10.9.2 Is your company legally compliant?

To ensure that your company is legally compliant with the relevant requirements, you should do the following:

1. Have a critical and careful look at your HIV/Aids policies and procedures (written documents), your workplace culture, and the typical reactions of management and your employees. Remember, everything you do must be based on human rights principles and comply with the law.

2. Ensure that your working environment protects the legal and human rights of all employees and that you reduce opportunities for possible discrimination and stigmatisation by
   - starting and supporting activities and programmes that make people aware of the rights of people living with HIV/Aids,
   - creating an HIV/Aids workplace policy that does not discriminate against people living with HIV/Aids, and
   - ensuring that none of your employee benefits discriminates against people living HIV/Aids.

3. Put mechanisms in place for dealing with human rights abuses and instances of discrimination.

4. If you feel that you do not have the resources to verify that your HIV/Aids policies and procedures are legally compliant, we encourage you to get advice from any of the following resources:

- the Aids Consortium,
- the Aids Law Project,
- the Aids Legal Network,
- the South African Human Rights Commission, and
- the Legal Aid Board.

Existing employees

HIV/Aids is not a notifiable disease and therefore employees who contract the disease are not obliged to inform the company. However, there is a duty to notify the company of incapacity or disability once an employee's health deteriorates to such an extent that he or she is unable to perform his or her duty in an adequate manner, or

- the disease manifests itself in excessive absenteeism, or
- the employee takes more than the standard amount of sick leave, or
- the employee displays irregular behaviour (e.g., Aids dementia).

Confidentiality

Persons living with HIV/Aids have the right to confidentiality and privacy concerning their health and HIV status. There should be no indicator on an employee's records if HIV status is known.

- All personal details of all employees, including the actual or suspected HIV status of any employee, shall remain strictly confidential.
- Any information about an employee's HIV status shall be revealed only with his or her written consent.
- An employee who contracts HIV will not be obligated to inform management. If an employee with HIV/Aids decides to disclose his or her diagnosis to a colleague, superior, or manager, the person will take all reasonable measures to ensure that this information remains private and confidential.
- The company will not tolerate any breaches in confidentiality. Any employee who breaches such confidentiality shall be subjected to appropriate disciplinary procedure. Speculation regarding another person's medical status will also not be tolerated.

Reasonable accommodation

Employees who become unfit for work as a result of Aids should be dealt with compassionately and in a just, humane, and life-affirming way. The company should attempt to reasonably accommodate such individuals in a less strenuous and stressful job, if possible. Failing this, the employee may be offered early retirement in accordance with standard company procedures and be entitled to appropriate benefits.

Employees at risk

The company should ensure that correct protective equipment is provided in all first-aid boxes and that employees are trained in the correct use of this equipment.

The company should ensure that all first-aid and healthcare workers are educated regarding HIV and Aids infections, as well as other potentially infectious diseases, and that they understand and adhere to these standard operating procedures.

Where necessary, the company will provide all relevant employees with appropriate protective clothing.

The risk of HIV infection from blood resulting from an injury is really small. However, you still need to ensure that employees who handle first aid are equipped to practice safe first aid and take appropriate precautions in line with health and safety legislation.

10.9.3 The World Health Organisation's guidelines

The World Health Organisation's (WHO) guidelines for basic HIV and Aids first aid are as follows:

- Wherever there is a risk of contact with body fluids, rubber/PVC gloves should be used for treatment of patients.
- If blood or body fluids get on to the skin, it should be thoroughly washed with soap and water. Bleach should not be used on the skin.
- Where heavy contamination is likely to be encountered, additional protection can be provided by use of a PVC apron. Eye protection should be worn.
- Where mouth-to-mouth resuscitation is required, plastic airways (Leadal) may be worn to reduce the risk of contamination from direct oral contact.

- Cuts or grazes should be covered with a waterproof dressing until scabs form.

- Spilt blood should be cleaned up, preferably by the person it came from, with strong household bleach diluted by 1 to 10 parts with water. For absolute safety, other body fluids should be treated in the same way.

- Tissues, dressings, and other contaminated materials should be tied up in heavy plastic bags/bin liners for disposal by incineration.

- Soiled sheets and clothing should be washed separately at a high temperature setting. Rubber/PVC gloves should be worn when handling soiled articles.

- Non-disposable instruments or receptacles used for treatment should be sterilised before re-use. Crockery and cutlery should be washed in hot water with detergent.

- Disposable needles and other 'sharps' should be placed in appropriate containers, which should be safely disposed of. Razors should not be re-used.

10.10 Self-evaluation

In terms of the legislative requirements governing workplace safely, what are your responsibilities as a small business owner in relation to

- safety representatives,
- health and safety committees,
- registering under the *Compensation for Occupational Injuries and Diseases Act*,
- specific safety regulations,
- general safety regulations,
- recording and reporting of accidents in the workplace, and
- recognising human rights with respect to HIV/Aids.

Employment equity and skills development

11.1 Learning outcomes

After you have studied this chapter, you should be able to

- identify whether you are a designated employer,

- identify and eliminate any forms of discrimination in your employment practices,

- explain the basic requirements for employment equity reporting if they are applicable to your business,

- register for levy payments with SARS,

- determine which SETA your business falls under,

- claim grants from your SETA if you qualify, and

- explain the functions and duties of a Skills Development Facilitator.

11.2 Background to employment equity

South Africa has had a legacy of discrimination on the basis of race, gender, and disability, which prevented the majority of citizens from obtaining access to opportunities for education, employment, promotion, and wealth creation. In addition, increased pressure on productivity and human resource development has required business to transform the old apartheid-style workplaces into organisations that are more representative of our population and provide equal opportunities to all.

As Jaque's business grows, she will have to keep a number of development issues in mind. If she trains her staff, will they end up with recognised skills? Does she employ the right profile of staff to reflect the demographics of the country? If she employs more and more staff, what developmental issues must she keep in mind? Does she have to pay any levies or submit any development plans or reports about how she is developing her staff? All these are governed by certain legislation so that the government can ensure that previously disadvantaged people are given advantages and are prioritised for development and subsequent sharing of wealth and economic benefits. If Jaque understands the legislation that promotes equity and development, she will be able to ensure that she develops her staff to their best advantage.

The fundamental principles for our employment equity and anti-discrimination legislation are contained in our Constitution.

11.2.1 The Constitution and employment equity

Chapter 2 of the *Constitution of the Republic of South Africa, Act 108 of 1996* contains the Bill of Rights, which entrenches certain fundamental rights for the citizens of the country. Section 9 of that chapter reads as follows:

Equality –

(1) Everyone is equal before the law and has the right to equal protection and benefit of the law.

(2) Equality includes the full and equal enjoyment of all rights and freedoms. To promote the achievement of equality, legislative and other measures designed to protect or advance persons, or categories of persons, disadvantaged by unfair discrimination, may be taken.

(3) The state may not unfairly discriminate directly or indirectly against anyone on one or more grounds, including race, gender, sex, pregnancy, marital status, ethnic or social origin, colour, sexual orientation, age, disability, religion, conscience, belief, culture, language or birth.

(4) No person may unfairly discriminate directly or indirectly against anyone on one or more grounds in terms of subsection (3). National legislation must be enacted to prevent or prohibit unfair discrimination.

(5) Discrimination on one or more of the grounds listed in subsection (3) is unfair unless it is established that the discrimination is fair.

From this section, it is clear that the Constitution relies on two mechanisms to eliminate discrimination:

- **Prohibition of discrimination**, through which the principle of equality of treatment is reinforced. This is called formal equality.
- **Affirmative action**, which is aimed at achieving equality in practice. Affirmative action aims at enshrining equality through the adoption of positive measures to empower previously disadvantaged persons.

It is against this constitutional framework that the two main pieces of legislation aimed at achieving equality and eradicating discrimination, the *Employment Equity Act, 55 of 1998*, and the *Promotion of Equality and Prevention of Unfair Discrimination Act, 4 of 2000*, were developed.

11.3   The Employment Equity Act, 55 of 1998

The Department of Labour introduced the *Employment Equity Act, 55 of 1998* (the EEA), which seeks to eliminate unfair discrimination in employment and provides for affirmative action to correct the imbalances of the past with respect to access to employment, training, promotion, and equitable remuneration, especially for black people, women, and the disabled. The department's website at www.labour.gov.za provides extensive information on employment equity including documents, formats, and guidelines.

The Act makes provision for employment equity plans for companies that employ more than 50 people or that meet a specific annual turnover threshold.

As most small businesses do not employ that many people, a number of the reporting requirements will not have to be met. However the Act covers a number of other issues such as the definition of an employee and discrimination in the workplace. This will be of value to small business owners.

An **employee** is regarded as any person, other than an independent contractor, who works for another person or for the state, and who receives or is entitled to receive remuneration. An employee also includes any person other than an independent contractor, who, in any manner, assists in carrying on or conducting the business of an employer. In terms of unfair discrimination, an applicant for a position is also regarded as an employee.

Temporary employment services: A person whose services are available to an employer who is required to submit an employment equity plan, by a temporary employment service (such as a company supplying casual banqueting staff to the hospitality industry), is considered to be an employee of that employer if the employment is of indefinite duration or for a period of three months or longer.

Where a temporary employment service, on the express or implied instructions of a client, commits an act of unfair discrimination, both the temporary employment service and the client are jointly and severally responsible.

11.4 Unfair discrimination

The EEA deals with the prohibition of unfair discrimination, and all employers and employees are required to comply.

No person may unfairly discriminate (directly or indirectly) against any employee or an applicant for employment on one or more grounds in any employment policy or practice, including race, gender, sex, pregnancy (or intended pregnancy, termination of pregnancy, or medical circumstances related to pregnancy), marital status, family responsibility (spouse or partner, dependent children, or immediate family members who need care and support), ethnic or social origin, colour, sexual orientation, age, disability, religion, HIV status, conscience, belief, political opinion, culture, language, and birth.

The following are some examples of unfair discrimination:

- **Medical testing**, including any test, question, inquiry, or other means designated to ascertain whether an employee has any medical condition, is prohibited. Medical testing may be conducted only under the following circumstances:
    - if legislation permits or requires the testing,
    - if it is justifiable in the light of medical facts, employment conditions, social policy, or the fair distribution of employee benefits, and
    - if the inherent requirements of the job demand it.
- **HIV testing:** Medical testing of an employee to determine HIV status is prohibited unless determined to be justifiable by the Labour Court.
- **Psychological testing** and any similar assessments are prohibited unless they can be scientifically shown to be valid and reliable, can be applied fairly to all employees, and are not biased against any particular employee or group of employees.
- **Harassment** of an employee, including sexual harassment, is also regarded as a form of unfair discrimination.

11.5 Affirmative action

Affirmative action refers to measures that are intended to ensure that suitably qualified employees from designated groups have equal employment opportunities and are equitably represented in all occupational categories and levels of the workforce.

These measures not only apply to the preferred appointment of members of designated groups, but also extend to the promotion, development, and training of employees to increase their prospects of advancement. In support of these measures, the employer may need to modify or adjust a job or the working environment.

These adjustments are likely to include

- identification and elimination of any barrier that impacts adversely on designated groups,

- measures that promote diversity,

- making reasonable accommodation for people from designated groups,

- retention, development, and training of designated groups (including skills development), and

- preferential treatment and numerical goals to ensure equitable representation. This excludes quotas.

Designated groups: The beneficiaries of affirmative action are persons from 'designated groups' who are 'suitably qualified' to benefit from affirmative action measures. The EEA defines 'designated groups' as

- 'black people', which is defined to mean Africans, coloureds, and Indians,

- women, and

- people with disabilities, who are 'people who have a long-term physical or mental impairment which substantially limits their prospects of entry into or advancement in, employment'.

A 'suitably qualified person' is defined as someone who may be qualified for a job as a result of any one (or a combination) of that person's formal qualifications, prior learning, and relevant experience, or his or her capacity to acquire, within reasonable time, the ability to do the job.

Discrimination on the ground of lack of relevant experience alone is considered to be unfair discrimination.

11.5.1 Designated employer

A designated employer means an employer who employs 50 or more employees, or has a total annual turnover as reflected in Schedule 4 of the Act. Employers can also volunteer to become designated employers.

Consider the categories listed below and determine if the turnover of your business exceeds the minimum requirements. If it does, then you are a designated employer and have to comply with the EEA reporting requirements.

The list below is taken from Schedule 4 of the EEA.

Sector	Total annual turnover
Agriculture	R2 million
Mining and quarrying	R7.5 million
Manufacturing	R10 million
Electricity, gas and water	R10 million
Construction	R5 million
Retail and motor trade and repair services	R15 million
Catering and accommodation	R5 million
Finance and business services	R10 million
Community, society and personal services	R5 million

11.5.2 Duties of a designated employer

If you qualify as a designated employer, you must implement affirmative action measures for designated groups to achieve employment equity.

Designated employers must

- consult with unions and employees in order to make sure that the EE plan is accepted by everybody,

- assign one or more senior managers to ensure implementation and monitoring of the employment equity plan and make available necessary resources for this purpose,
- conduct an analysis of all employment policies, practices, and procedures and prepare a profile of their workforce to identify any problems relating to employment equity (discussed in detail below),
- prepare and implement an employment equity plan setting out the affirmative action measures they intend taking to achieve employment equity goals (discussed in detail below),
- report to the director-general on progress made in the implementation of the employment equity plan, and
- display in the workplace a summary of the provisions of the EEA in all languages relevant to their workforce.

Consultation

Designated employers are required to take reasonable steps to consult with employees regarding workplace analysis, the preparation and implementation of an employment equity plan, and the submission and subsequent reporting on the employment equity plan to the director-general.

Consultation with employees must take place

- with a representative of the trade union representing members at the workplace and its employees or representatives nominated by them, or
- if no representative trade union represents members at the workplace, with employees directly or representatives nominated by them.

Employees or their nominated representative must include

- employees across all occupational categories and levels in the organisation,
- employees from designated groups, and
- employees not from designated groups.

The designated employer must disclose to the consulting parties all relevant information that will allow those parties to consult effectively.

Transparency/duty to inform

> All employers must display at the workplace, where it can be read by all employees, a notice, in the prescribed form, informing employees about the provisions of the Act. A poster of the EEA can be obtained from the Department of Labour.

In each of its workplaces, a designated employer must place in prominent, accessible places

- the most recent employment equity report submitted,
- any compliance order, arbitration award or order of the labour court concerning the provisions of this Act in relation to the employer, and
- any other document concerning this Act as prescribed.

Employment analysis

Designated employers must conduct an analysis of employment policies, practices, procedures, and working environment to identify any employment barriers that may negatively affect members of designated groups. The analysis must also include the development of a workforce profile to determine to what extent designated groups are under-represented in the workplace.

The analysis must be conducted in order to

- identify employment barriers that adversely affect people from designated groups,
- identify the degree of under-representation of people from designated groups in each occupational category and level in the workforce, and
- review employment policies and practices including, but not limited to,
  - recruitment procedures, advertising, and selection criteria,
  - appointments and the appointment process,
  - job classification and grading,
  - remuneration, employment benefits, and terms and conditions of employment,
  - job assignments,
  - the working environment and facilities,
  - training and development,

- ○ performance evaluation system,
- ○ promotion,
- ○ transfer,
- ○ demotion,
- ○ disciplinary measures other than dismissal, and
- ○ dismissal.

11.5.3 Preparing an employment equity plan

An employment equity (EE) plan must contain

- objectives for each year of the plan,

- affirmative action measures,

- numerical goals for achieving equitable representation,

- a timetable for each year,

- internal monitoring and evaluation procedures, and

- the names of the persons who will monitor and implement the EE plan.

The EE plan must state

- the duration of the plan, which may not be shorter than one year or longer than five years,
- the objectives to be achieved for each year of the plan, and
- the affirmative action measures to be implemented, which would include
  - ○ measures to identify and eliminate employment barriers, including unfair discrimination that might adversely affect people from designated groups,
  - ○ measures designed to further diversity in the workplace,
  - ○ making reasonable accommodation for people from designated groups to ensure that they enjoy equal opportunities and are equitably represented in the workforce,
  - ○ preferential treatment and numerical goals (not quotas) to ensure the equitable representation of suitably qualified people from designated groups in all occupational categories and levels in the workforce,
  - ○ measures to retain and develop people from designated groups and to implement appropriate training, including any measures in terms of any legislation providing for skills development.

Where an analysis reveals an under-representation of people from designated groups, the EE plan must state the numerical goals to achieve equitable representation of suitably qualified people from the designated groups within each occupational category and level, the timetable to achieve this desired state, and the strategies intended to achieve the goals.

This analysis should use the same factors that the Department of Labour will use to assess compliance. These factors are

- the demographic profile of the national and regionally economically active population,
- the pool of suitably qualified people from designated groups from which the employer may reasonably be expected to promote or appoint employees,
- the economic and financial factors relevant to the sector in which the employer operates,
- the present and anticipated economic and financial circumstances of the employer, and
- the number of present and planned vacancies that exist in the various categories and levels, as well as the employer's labour turnover.

The EE plan must also state

- the procedures that will be used to monitor and evaluate the implementation of the plan and whether reasonable progress is being made towards implementing employment equity,
- internal dispute-resolution procedures regarding any dispute about the interpretation and implementation of the plan,
- the persons, including one or more senior managers, with due authority and means, responsible for monitoring and implementing the plan, and
- any other prescribed matter.

A designated employer is not required to take any decision concerning employment policy or practice that would establish an absolute barrier to the prospective or continued employment or advancement of people who are *not* from designated groups.

11.5.4 Reporting

Designated employers must submit reports to the Department of Labour, as follows:

- Designated employers employing fewer than 150 people must submit a report every two years on the first working day of October.
- A designated employer employing 150 or more people has to submit a report annually on the first working day of October.

The first EE report to the Department of Labour deals with the detail of the initial development of and consultation around the plan. Subsequent reports detail the progress made with regards the implementation of the plan. The submission schedule for employment equity reports is summarised in the table below.

Employer	When to submit	How often
<150 employees	1 October	Every two years
>150 employees	1 October	Annually

Any small business that is established and grows in terms of its annual turnover and employment number must be aware that, once the requirements as a designated employer have been met, they will have to meet the provisions of the EEA in terms of submission of an EE plan and subsequent EE reports on the implementation of the EE plan.

The EE report is a public document. The employer is therefore required to display a copy of the most recent report in all workplaces. Public companies are also required to publish a summary of the EE report in their annual financial reports.

11.5.5 Awarding of state contracts

Designated employers who want to enter into commercial contracts/tenders with organs of the state must comply with the provisions of the EEA. The Minister of Labour will issue a time-limited certificate confirming the relevant compliance which you may attach to your tender application. Alternatively, you may attach a declaration of compliance that has been verified by the director-general.

Explain or define each of the following:

- Employment equity,
- Discrimination,
- Medical testing,

- Psychological testing,

- Harassment,

- Affirmative action,

- Designated groups,

- Designated employer,

- Consultation,

- Transparency, and

- Prohibition.

11.6   Codes of Good Practice

The Minister of Labour has issued Codes of Good Practice to provide employers with information and guidance that may help them in the implementation of the Act. These are available from the Department of Labour or may be found on their website.

The codes include

- preparing employment equity plans,
- advertising, recruitment procedures, and selection criteria,
- special measures to be taken in relation to persons with family responsibilities and to persons with disabilities, including benefit schemes,
- practice on key aspects of HIV/Aids and employment,
- sexual and racial harassment,
- internal dispute-resolution procedures regarding the interpretation or application of the Act, and sector-specific issues, and
- guidelines to employers on the prioritisation of specific designated groups.

11.6.1   Reporting to the Department of Labour

Employment equity reports using form (EEA2), together with the Income Differential Statement using Form EEA4, must be submitted to the Department of Labour. Both forms are available from the department or online. They must be submitted to the Employment Equity Registry, Department of Labour, Pretoria, or to the provincial office or labour centre in an envelope clearly marked 'Employment Equity Registry'.

| tip | Keep a copy of the report, as well as a record that the report was sent. The onus will be on you to prove that the report was submitted. Registered mail is a safe option for submitting your report in hard copy. |

Designated employers whose operations extend across different geographical areas, functional units, workplaces, or sectors may elect to submit either a consolidated or a separate report for each. This decision should be made by employers after consultation with the relevant stakeholders.

Below is a table to check compliance with the provisions of the EEA and Regulations.

Who	What	When
Department of Labour	• Enforcement and inspection	• Continuous, planned, and unplanned
Designated employers	• Consult with unions and employees in order to make sure that the EE plan is accepted by everybody • Assign one or more senior managers to ensure implementation and monitoring of the employment equity plan and make necessary resources available for this purpose • Conduct an analysis of all employment policies, practices, and procedures and prepare a profile of the workforce to identify any problems relating to employment equity • Prepare and implement an employment equity plan setting out the affirmative action measures they intend taking to achieve employment equity goals • Report to the director-general on progress made in the implementation of the EE plan • Display a summary of the provisions of the EEA in all languages relevant to their workforce	• Continuous and annually
Designated employers	**Less than 150 employees:** • Develop and submit EE plan to Department of Labour – duration 1 to 5 years • Submit EE Implementation Report Plan to Department of Labour to report on the implementation of the plan as stipulated	• Submit EE plan when previous plan expires • Submit EE report every two years on the 1st working day of October

Who	What	When
	More than 150 employees • Develop and submit EE plan to Department of Labour – duration 1 to 5 years • Submit EE plan to Department of Labour – report on the implementation of the plan as stipulated	• Submit EE plan when previous plan expires • Submit EE Report every year on 1st working day of October

11.7 The Promotion of Equality and Prevention of Unfair Discrimination Act

The *Promotion of Equality and Prevention of Unfair Discrimination Act, 4 of 2000* supplements the EEA in so far as equality and anti-discrimination legislation in South Africa is concerned. The difference is that the EEA has application specifically in the workplace, whereas the *Promotion of Equality and Prevention of Unfair Discrimination Act* applies generally.

11.7.1 Purpose of the Act

The objectives of this Act are specifically to

* enact legislation required by section 9 of the Constitution,

* give effect to the letter and spirit of the Constitution, in particular:

    * the equal enjoyment of all rights and freedoms by every person,

    * the promotion of equality,

    * the values of non-racialism and non-sexism, and

    * the prevention of advocacy of hatred based on race, ethnicity, gender, or religion;

* provide for measures to facilitate the eradication of unfair discrimination, hate speech, and harassment, particularly on the grounds of race, gender, and disability,

* provide procedures for the determination of circumstances under which discrimination is unfair,

* provide measures to educate the public and raise awareness of the importance of promoting equality and overcoming unfair discrimination, hate speech, and harassment,

* provide remedies for victims of unfair discrimination, hate speech, and harassment and persons whose right to equality has been infringed, and

* facilitate compliance with international law obligations in terms of specified conventions which focus on the subject matter of this Act.

11.7.2 Application of the Act

The Act binds both the state and all of the citizens of South Africa. The Promotion of Equality and Prevention of Unfair Discrimination Act is an Act of general application in contrast to the EEA, which is focused specifically on the workplace.

11.7.3 Provisions of the Act

Prohibitions

The state and any person is prohibited from unfairly discriminating against any other person. The Act imposes a burden on all citizens as well as the state not to discriminate unfairly, and at the same time protects everyone against unfair discrimination. The grounds on which unfair discrimination is prohibited are race, gender, disability, and hate speech.

Procedure and enforcement

The key mechanism to enforce the provisions of the Act is by means of legal action on the part of the aggrieved party in court. Existing magistrate's courts and High Courts will adjudicate matters related to the Act.

The Act has a unique feature regarding a person's right to institute legal action in a particular matter. The normal rule is that a person can only institute legal action in respect of his or her own right, and not on behalf of anyone else, unless they have power of attorney for another person. However, this Act provides that proceedings may be instituted by

* any person acting in his or her own interest – the normal rule,
* any person acting on behalf of another person who cannot act in their own name,
* any person acting as a member of, or in the interest of, a group or class of people,
* any person acting in the public interest, and
* the South African Human Rights Commission or the Commission for Gender Equality.

11.7.4 Illustrative list of unfair practices

The schedule attached to the Act contains a list of practices that illustrate what would be considered as an unfair or discriminatory practice. For example, the following would all be regarded as unfair:

* **Labour and employment:** failure to respect a principle of equal pay for equal work.

* **Healthcare services and benefits:** subjecting people to medical experiments or tests without their informed consent.

* **Education:** failure to reasonably and practicably accommodate diversity.

* **Housing, accommodation, land, and property:** arbitrary eviction of people on one or more prohibited grounds.

* **Insurance services:** disadvantaging a person, including unfairly and unreasonably refusing to grant services to persons solely on HIV/Aids status.

* **Partnerships:** imposing unfair and discriminatory terms or conditions under which a person is invited to become a partner.

* **Professional bodies:** unfairly limiting or denying members access to benefits or facilities on prohibited grounds.

* **Provision of goods, services, and facilities:** the practice of unfairly limiting access to contractual opportunities for supplying goods and services.

* **Clubs, sports, and associations:** failure to promote diversity in selection of representative teams.

1. What is the difference between discrimination and affirmative action?

2. Explain the process of reporting on the achievement of employment equity.

3. Can you identify any practices in your business that may unwittingly discriminate against anyone?

4. Are you are a designated employer and, if so, when do you have to submit your EE Plan?

11.8 Skills development

The South African government has committed itself to development of the labour force through the *Skills Development Act, 97 of 1998* and the *Skills Development Levies Act, 9 of 1999*. These two pieces of legislation introduce new institutions, programmes, and funding policies designed to increase investment in skills development.

The *Skills Development Act* promotes the development and improvement of employee skills. The Act further requires that employers pay a Skills Development Levy. This compulsory levy is covered in the *Skills Development Levies Act of 1999*, which outlines the details of who should pay the levy and what amounts should be paid.

Regulations promulgated under both of these Acts provide the operational and logistical means of achieving their objectives.

11.8.1 How is the levy calculated?

The levy is one percent of the 'leviable amount', this being 'the total amount of remuneration, paid or payable, or deemed to be paid or payable, by an employer to its employees during any month'.

The following items are included:

* normal salary, wages, overtime pay, bonus, gratuity, commission, and leave pay, etc.,
* remuneration paid to employees who do not have to pay tax; i.e., their remuneration falls below the income tax threshold,
* pensions and retirement allowances,
* fifty percent of travelling allowances,
* fifty percent of any allowances to holders of public office, and
* fringe benefits valued in terms of the *Income Tax Act* (Schedule 7).

The following are excluded:

* lump sums from pension, provident, and retirement annuity funds,
* amounts payable to a learner in terms of a contract of employment (as defined in the *Skills Development Act*),
* amounts paid to independent consultants or labour brokers,
* reimbursed allowances, e.g. entertainment or travel allowances, and
* amounts paid to non-executive directors of private companies.

11.8.2 Who has to pay the levy - when and to whom?

The levy must be paid by every employer who is

* registered with the South African Revenue Services (SARS) for PAYE, even if they only pay PAYE for a single employee, and/or
* has an annual payroll in excess of R500 000.

Employers are required to pay the levy to SARS, no later than seven days after the end of each month.

11.8.3 How do employers register for payment of the levy?

From May 2003, SARS introduced a statement of account (EMP2) integrating the following three aspects in respect of SDL payments:

* acknowledgement of payment received (IRP/UIF/SDL213),
* final demand to submit a return EMP201 (EMP 204), and
* final demand for payment of outstanding amount/additional penalty/penalty/ interest (EMP208).

While only some employers have to pay the levy, every employer must register as an employer with SARS. This is so that the appropriate Sector Education Training Authority (SETA) has a record of every employer in the sector, whether or not it is exempt from paying the levy.

Levy registration forms (SDL 101) and 'Employer Guidelines to Registration' (SDL10) are obtainable from any SARS office or from their website (www.sars.gov.za). If an organisation has a number of branches or sites, an additional registration form (SDL 102) must be completed for each branch or site.

11.8.4 Exemptions from paying the levy

While every employer must register with SARS, the following employers can apply for exemption from paying the levy:

* employers whose payroll is less than R500 000 per year and who are not required to register for PAYE,
* any public service employer in the national or provincial sphere,
* national or provincial public entities, if eighty percent or more of their expenditure is defrayed directly or indirectly from funds voted by Parliament,

* any municipality in possession of a certificate of exemption from the Minister of Labour,

* religious or charitable institutions, or any fund that is exempt from the payment of income tax.

The application for exemption is contained in the SDL101 form, which is also available from any SARS office or from their website.

If your business has a payroll of less than R500 000 per year, you must register with SARS, and then apply for exemption from the Skills Development Levy.

11.9   How are levies allocated and what can be claimed?

The allocation of levies is set out below:

National Skills Fund (NSF) For priority projects for national skills development	18%
SARS For administration of the collection of levies	2%
The relevant SETA	80% 10% for administrative and operational costs. 70% is available as grants to employers who paid the levy and met the criteria for grants.

11.9.1 What can employers claim from levies paid?

Grants are payments made by SETAs to employers in the sector who have met the criteria for various categories of grant. Employers may claim grants of up to seventy percent of the levy they have paid. There are two kinds of grant: mandatory grants and discretionary grants.

Mandatory grants are paid by SETAs when employers who pay the levy meet the established requirements and these are approved by the SETA. The mandatory grant of fifty percent is payable in four quarterly payments on the SETA's approval of the Workplace Skills Plan (including the nomination of the Skills Development Facilitator) and the Implementation Report.

Discretionary grants are paid to employers who implement skills initiatives that are usually in addition to those in the Workplace Skills Plan and that are defined in terms of the SETA Grant Regulations issued in July 2005.

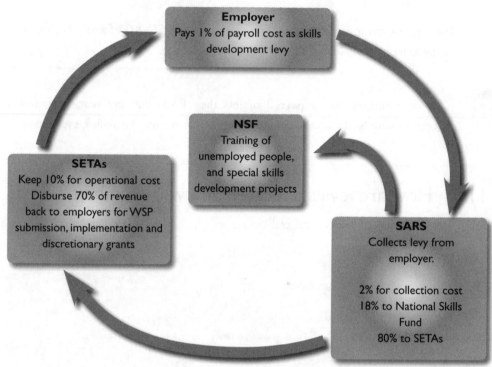

Figure 11.1 Levy and grant process established by the Skills Development Levies Act

Employers cannot claim grants against the cost of training implemented, only grants in proportion to the skills levies paid.

Grant	% Employer's Levy	Due date for submitting application
Mandatory grants: Workplace Skills Plan Implementation Report	50%	The Workplace Skills Plan must be submitted on or before 30 June each year, along with the Implementation Report for the previous Workplace SkillsPlan.
Discretionary grants: Refer to each SETA for criteria	20%	
Total available for grants	70%	

11.10 How to apply for grants

11.10.1 Qualifying for mandatory grants

To qualify for mandatory grants, levy-paying employers must be registered with the SETA and their levy payments must be up to date.

To ensure that the SETA has the correct information from SARS and that it meets the demands of the Auditor–General, and to ensure that employers get the correct grant payments, all the SETA levy-paying employers are required to complete the EMP201 page on the SETA SMS database. This page allows the employer to complete the same information as required on the SARS EMP 201, and will include the following information:

- financial year,
- date paid,
- for which month, and
- amount paid.

Employers may fax or email a scanned copy of the monthly SARS EMP 201 form to the SETA on a monthly basis. Check the requirements with your SETA.

This will assist the SETA in paying the grants in good time by enabling the reconciliation of accounts that might otherwise delay the payment.

11.11 Skills Development Facilitators

11.11.1 What is a Skills Development Facilitator?

The Skills Development Facilitator (SDF) is responsible for the development and planning of an organisation's skills development strategy for a specific period. This includes the development and implementation of an annual Workplace Skills Plan, the submission of an Annual Training Report/Implementation Report, and Discretionary Grant applications.

He or she also serves as a resource to the employer about

- conducting analyses of skills audits/skills needs,
- the criteria required for accreditation as a Training Provider, and
- the application for and implementation of Learnerships.

11.11.2 What are the functions of a Skills Development Facilitator?

The SDF is responsible for

- assisting the employer to become registered with the SETA,
- assisting the employer and employees with the development of a Workplace Skills Plan (WSP),
- submitting the WSP to the SETA,
- advising the employer on the implementation of the WSP,
- assisting the employer with the drafting of an Annual Training Report/ Implementation Report against the approved WSP,
- formulating training practice to comply with Discretionary Grant requirements,
- submitting applications for Discretionary Grants,
- advising the employer on the SETA's quality assurance requirements with regard to accreditation as a workplace Training Provider.
- serving as a contact person between the employer and the SETA, and
- providing the SETA with additional information that may be required.

11.11.3 Who can be appointed as a Skills Development Facilitator?

- A Skills Development Facilitator (SDF) can be
- an employee,
- a formally contracted, external person, or
- a person who is jointly employed by a number of other employers to assess the skills development needs of the group of employers and employees concerned.

11.11.4 What can employers gain by appointing and using a Skills Development Facilitator?

Businesses that pay the skills levy may claim up to 70 per cent of their levies back in grants if the SDF submits grant applications in accordance with the prescribed requirements.

11.12 Workplace Skills Plans

A Workplace Skills Plan (WSP) is a plan – approved by the SETA – that outlines the training and development for an organisation for one year.

Information required by a Workplace Skills Plan includes

- the number of people trained in the organisation by job type and race,
- the organisation's strategic priorities for skills development,
- the training and education needed to ensure the development of the business and employees,
- details of the education and training needed to achieve these priorities, including proposed training interventions, estimated costs, specific job types, and whether interventions will be conducted by external training providers or the organisation itself, and
- information regarding employment equity in the organisation.

11.12.1 Purpose of the Workplace Skills Plan

Workplace Skills Plans can impact positively on a number of areas within an organisation:

- management and employees start to discuss skills in the workplace,
- gaps and shortfalls in skills required are identified and positive ways of addressing them are devised,
- the organisation uncovers talents and skills it did not know it had, and
- management shares the organisation's goals with employees, who are then better able to understand them and commit themselves to the process of achieving them.

Apart from these benefits, the Implementation Grant – which is a percentage of the levy paid by organisations to the SETA – will be paid to organisations that show that they have implemented plans identified in their Workplace Skills Plan.

11.12.2 Compiling a Workplace Skills Plan

The Skills Development Facilitator is formally responsible for submitting the Workplace Skills Plan to the SETA, and plays a major role in its compilation.

When compiling a Workplace Skills Plan, an organisation should

- consider its goals and priorities for the year for which the WSP is being drafted and plan training to address these,
- refer to its business plan,
- incorporate information obtained from any career-pathing exercises, skills audits, or processes in which individual training needs are identified,
- refer to its Employment Equity Plan, as many of the information fields are the same, and
- consult extensively with its Workplace Training Committee or Employment Equity Committee (many organisations have one committee that serves both functions) to determine the requirements of both labour and management.

11.12.3 Implementing and reporting on the Workplace Skills Plan

Organisations should keep records of all the training, activities, assessment, and/or development initiatives implemented according to the WSP in preparation for preparing implementation report(s) for the reporting period. Organisations must submit an Implementation Report, with supporting documentation, to qualify for mandatory grants in the following scheme year.

The Skills Development Facilitator must prepare these reports, listing all the interventions implemented according to the WSP.

11.12.4 Supporting documents/evidence of implementation of the Workplace Skills Plan

Evidence in support of the implementation of the Workplace Skills Plan must be submitted to the SETA on or before the submission date (30 June annually) of the Implementation Plan.

Examples of suitable supporting evidence include

- attendance registers signed by learners,
- copies of invoices and payments to training providers, and
- copies of attendance and competence certificates.

11.13 Workplace Training Committees

It is a legislated requirement in terms of the various skills development legislation that employers of 50 or more employees form a Workplace Training Committee representing both owner/employer and labour/employee interests.

The committee must meet regularly to collectively determine training priorities, agree on skills gaps and subsequent interventions to be implemented, and so on.

Many employers combine the functions and objectives of an employment equity committee and a training committee, as the issues discussed overlap considerably. This arrangement makes it more practical for employers by minimising time away from work for participating members.

11.13.1 SETA requirements regarding a Workplace Training Committee

Businesses that employ 50 persons or more must ensure that a Workplace Training Committee is properly constituted to adequately represent the interests of both management and labour. They must

- ensure that committee members are capacitated on the role, function, and objectives of the forum,
- ensure that the committee meets regularly to deliberate relevant issues and make decisions on all skills development issues,
- keep detailed minutes of all meetings held, and
- keep signed copies of attendance registers from the meetings.

11.13.2 Functions of the Training Committee

- Develop a training policy.
- Ensure that the development and implementation of the Workplace Skills Plan is aligned to the strategic mission and vision of the company.
- Keep the envisaged training and development of employees in the company abreast with the long-term transformation objectives of the company.
- Ensure that the Workplace Skills Plan is aligned to the Employment Equity Plan and business plan of a company.

- Establish training priorities for the company based on its short- and long-term needs.
- Align training to the Sector Skills Plan, learnerships, career pathways, accredited national qualifications, etc.
- Support the SDF in communicating the completed Workplace Skills Plan to other employees in the company.
- Monitor the implementation of the Workplace Skills Plan.
- Revise the Workplace Skills Plan periodically. This will in most cases be carried out in conjunction with the training committee.

Compile the annual Training Implementation Report.

The following is a list of Sector Education and Training Authorities (SETAs):

- **AGRISETA:** Agriculture Sector Education and Training Authority
- **BANKSETA:** Banking Sector Education and Training Authority
- **CETA:** Construction Education and Training Authority
- **CHIETA:** Chemical Industries Education and Training Authority
- **CTFL:** Clothing, Textiles, Footwear and Leather SETA
- **ESETA:** Energy Sector Education and Training Authority
- **ETDP:** Education, Training and Development Practices SETA
- **FASSET:** Financial and Accounting Services SETA
- **FIETA:** Forest Industries Education and Training Authority
- **FOODBEV:** Food and Beverages Manufacturing Industry SETA
- **HWSETA:** Health and Welfare SETA
- **INSETA:** Insurance Sector Education and Training Authority
- **ISETT:** Information Systems Electronics & Telecommunication Technologies
- **LGSETA:** Local Government Sector Education and Training Authority
- **MAPPP SETA:** Media, Advertising, Publishing, Printing and Packaging SETA
- **MERSETA:** Manufacturing, Engineering and Related Services SETA
- **MQA:** Mining Qualifications Authority
- **PSETA:** Public Service SETA
- **SASSETA:** Safety and Security Sector Education & Training Authority
- **SERVICES SETA:** Services Sector Education and Training Authority
- **TETA:** Transport Education and Training Authority

- **THETA:** Tourism and Hospitality and Sport Education and Training Authority
- **W & R SETA:** Wholesale and Retail SETA

11.14 Self-evaluation

1. Write a job specification and job description for a Skills Development Facilitator.

2. Design a process for the development of a Workplace Skills Plan.

3. Describe how skills development and employment equity are complimentary principles and processes.

4. Explain the rationale and process of the levy-grant system to a friend who intends starting a business.

References

Du Plessis, L. 1999. An introduction to law. Third edition. Cape Town: Juta & Co, Ltd.

Gordon-Davis/Cumberlege – 2004. Legal Requirements for South African Students & Practitioners. Cape Town. Juta & Co Ltd

Gordon-Davis, L. 1998. The hospitality industry handbook on hygiene and safety for South African students and practitioners. Cape Town: Juta & Co, Ltd.

Havenga, P, et al. 2002. General principles of commercial law. Cape Town: Juta & Co, Ltd.

Kleyn, D and Viljoen, F. 2002 Beginners' guide for law students. Third edition. Cape Town: Juta & Co, Ltd.

Moolman, M. 2002. Module 2: Getting to grips with the legal aspects of your guest house. Sunday Times Bed & Breakfast Training Manual.

Sinclair-Hughes, S. 2003. Workplace relations and industry legislation. Rondebosch: Varsity College.

Strydom, JW, Nieuwenhuizen, C, Le Roux, EE, and Jacobs, H (eds). 1996. Entrepreneurship and how to establish your own business. Cape Town: Juta & Co, Ltd.

Thomas, A, and Robertshaw, D. 1999. Achieving employment equity: A guide to effective strategies. Johannesburg: Knowledge Resources.

Vrancken, PHG, et al. 2002. Tourism and the law in South Africa. Durban: Butterworths

STATUTES

General Hygiene Requirements for Food Premises and the Transport of Food Regulations R918 of July 1999.

MOS Act General Safety Regulation R1031.

Regional Services Council Act No 109 of 1995

General Safety Regulations: Regulation 1031 of 30 May 1986.

The Basic Conditions of Employment Act 75 of 1997

The Business Act 71 of 1991

The Close Corporations Act 69 of 1984

The Companies Act 61 of 1973

The Compensation for Occupational Injuries and Diseases Act 130 of 1993

The Constitution of South Africa Act 108 of 1996

The Credit Agreements Act 75 of 1980

The Employment Equity Act 55 of 1998,

The Environmental Conservation Act 73 of 1989

The Financial Intelligence Centre Act 38 of 2001

The Health Act 63 of 1977

The Income Tax Act 58 of 1962

The Insolvency Act 24 of 1936

The Labour Relations Act 66 of 1995

The Law of Evidence Amendment Act 45 of 1988

The Liquor Act 27 of 1989

The Local Government Transitional Act of 1995

The Long-term Insurance Act 52 of 1998

The National Building Regulations as applied through SABS 0400

The National Gambling Act 33 of 1996

The National Land Transport Transition Act 22 of 2000

The National Roads Act 7 of 1998

The National Water Act 36 of 1998

The Occupational Health and Safety Act 85 of 1993

The Rental Housing Act 21 of 1999

The Short-term Insurance Act 53 of 1998

The Skills Development Act 97 of 1998

The Skills Development Levies Act 9 of 1999

The Standards Act 30 of 1982

The Unemployment Insurance Act 63 of 2001

The Unemployment Insurance Contributions Act, 4 of 2002

The Usury Act 73 of 1968

The Broad-Based Black Economic Empowerment Act, 53 of 2003

The Small Business Act, 102 of 1996

The Tobacco Products Control Act, 83 of 1993

WEBSITES

SA Government - National Departments

Environmental Affairs & Tourism

Government Communications (GCIS)

Health

Justice & Constitutional Development

Labour

Land Affairs

National Treasury

SA Revenue Service

Trade & Industry

Transport

Water Affairs & Forestry